ISBN 978-0-259-31385-4
PIBN 10813440

1 MONTH OF
FREE
READING

at

www.ForgottenBooks.com

By purchasing this book you are eligible for one month membership to ForgottenBooks.com, giving you unlimited access to our entire collection of over 1,000,000 titles via our web site and mobile apps.

To claim your free month visit:

www.forgottenbooks.com/free813440

COLLECTION

OF

BRITISH AUTHORS

TAUCHNITZ EDITION.

VOL. 1751.

A POETRY-BOOK OF MODERN POETS

(SECOND SERIES)

SELECTED AND ARRANGED BY

AMELIA B. EDWARDS.

A POETRY-BOOK
OF MODERN POETS

CONSISTING OF

SONGS & SONNETS, ODES & LYRICS

SELECTED AND ARRANGED, WITH NOTES,

FROM THE WORKS OF THE MODERN ENGLISH
AND AMERICAN POETS,

DATING FROM THE MIDDLE
OF THE EIGHTEENTH CENTURY TO THE PRESENT TIME;

BY

AMELIA B. EDWARDS.

COPYRIGHT EDITION.

LEIPZIG

BERNHARD TAUCHNITZ

1878.

TO THE READER.

THIS Poetry-Book of Modern Poets begins, as to date, with Robert Burns and ends with the poets of to-day. Burns marks, in fact, the great starting-point of contemporary poetry. Between him and his immediate predecessors there is fixed a great gulf, as of a century of time; while for modernness of thought and style, and for simple expression of feeling, all that he has given us might have been written yesterday. With him, therefore, although he died four years before the commencement of our century, the present school of English poetry is assumed to begin.

As in the preceding volume, no chronological order has been observed in the arrangement of the poems; the position of each piece being determined solely by its relation to that which leads up to it or follows it. Thus Shelley and Jean Ingelow, Swinburne and Coleridge, as they may illustrate or contrast with each other, will be found side by side. In this way (to quote the Preface printed with the Poetry-Book of Elder Poets) "it is hoped that readers who care to observe the attitude of contemporary thought on certain universal subjects, such as Love, or Death, or the Influences of Nature, will like to find grouped together poems which treat of a common theme. These groups, again, are for the most part linked with other groups in such wise as to carry on slight chains of connection between subjects far apart. By bringing together, for instance, songs of courtship, of lullaby, of childish growth and promise, of early death and of parental bereavement, it has been sought to convey something like an episodical picture of everyday human life. To the few who may be interested in tracing them, these lines of association may perhaps convey an added sense of harmony; while for those who prefer dipping into the book wherever it may chance to open, each poem will have its individual and unassisted charm.

"Here and there, to suggest the intended sequence, the Editor, following the precedent of Mr. F. T. Palgrave, has ventured, though with all diffidence, to give or alter a title. It may be as well to observe, however, that readers who desire to take the poets in strict order of succession may do so by referring to the Table of Authors, which has been chronologically arranged for that purpose.

"The notes at the end of the volume are given, not in the vain hope of offering anything new in the way of criticism, but in order to assist foreign readers, and to supply the place of those classical and other dictionaries which travellers are obliged to leave at home." *Preface to A Poetry-Book of Elder Poets.*

Touching the general contents of this volume, it will be easily understood that the duty of levying contributions from the works of living authors must have largely added to the difficulty of the task. Herein, however, the Editor has endeavoured to be as little as possible biassed by merely personal taste, and as far as possible guided by contemporary and popular verdict. For the rest, the whole field of modern English Poetry has been surveyed and gleaned to fill the following pages. No famous name will, it is believed, be found unrepresented; and some few names which are less known than they deserve to be (as, for instance, that of Thomas Lovell Beddoes) will here be met with for almost the first time in a work of this character. Certain American poets with whom, to our loss, we are but too slightly acquainted, have also received due recognition. It is, indeed, difficult to see how any selection that includes writers still living can be deemed complete without them.

The Editor, in conclusion, takes this opportunity of tendering her thanks to the Lord Houghton, Matthew Arnold Esq., William Morris Esq., A. C. Swinburne Esq., J. A. Symonds Esq., and Miss Christina Rossetti, for the ready permission by which certain of their poems appear in the following pages. Also to Robert Buchanan Esq. who has himself most kindly abridged his poem "The Storm," in order to bring it within the necessary compass. Messrs. Longmans & Co., Macmillan & Co., and Smith, Elder & Co., have with the like courtesy conceded some copyright verses by Macaulay, Southey, the late Canon Kingsley, and G. Macdonald Esq., while Mrs. Clough has granted the use of two poems from the pen of the late Arthur Hugh Clough. The fine poem entitled "In the Storm" by the late Mrs. Norton, was presented to the Editor, expressly for this work, by the author, and has till now, it is believed, existed only in a privately printed form, and in MS.

AMELIA B. EDWARDS.

Westbury on Trym,
Gloucestershire, 1878.

CONTENTS.

———

CONTENTS.

CONTENTS.

MODERN ENGLISH POETS.

JOHN ANDERSON.

JOHN ANDERSON my jo, John,
When we were first acquent
Your locks were like the raven,
Your bonnie brow was brent;
But now your brow is bald, John,
Your locks are like the snow;
But blessings on your frosty pow,
John Anderson my jo.

John Anderson my jo, John,
We clamb the hill thegither,
And mony a canty day, John,
We've had wi' ane anither:
Now we maun totter down, John,
But hand in hand we'll go,
And sleep thegither at the foot,
John Anderson my jo.

Robert Burns.

I *

OH, WERT THOU IN THE CAULD BLAST.

OH, wert thou in the cauld blast
　On yonder lea, on yonder lea,
My plaidie to the angry airt,
　I'd shelter thee, I'd shelter thee:
Or did misfortune's bitter storms
　Around thee blaw, around thee blaw,
Thy bield should be my bosom
　To share it a', to share it a'.

Or were I in the wildest waste,
　Sae bleak and bare, sae bleak and bare,
The desert were a paradise
　If thou wert there, if thou wert there:
Or were I monarch o' the globe,
　Wi' thee to reign, wi' thee to reign,
The brightest jewel in my crown
　Wad be my queen, wad be my queen

R. Burns.

O MY LUVE'S LIKE A RED, RED ROSE.

O MY Luve's like a red, red rose
　That's newly sprung in June:
O my Luve's like the melodie
　That's sweetly play'd in tune.
As fair art thou, my bonnie lass,
　So deep in luve am I:
And I will luve thee still, my dear,
　Till a' the seas gang dry:

Till a' the seas gang dry, my Dear,
　And the rocks melt wi' the sun;
I will luve thee still, my dear,
　While the sands o' life shall run.
And fare thee weel, my only Luve!
　And fare thee weel a while!
And I will come again, my Luve,
　Tho' it were ten thousand mile.

R. Burns.

MY JEAN.

OF a' the airts the wind can blaw,
   I dearly like the west,
For there the bonnie lassie lives,
   The lassie I lo'e best:
There wild woods grow, and rivers row,
   And mony a hill between;
But, day and night, my fancy's flight
   Is ever wi' my Jean.

I see her in the dewy flowers,
   I see her sweet and fair:
I hear her in the tunefu' birds,
   I hear her charm the air:
There's not a bonnie flower that springs
   By fountain, shaw, or green;
There's not a bonnie bird that sings,
   But minds me o' my Jean.

R. Burns.

ELEU LORO.

WHERE shall the lover rest
   Whom the fates sever
From his true maiden's breast
   Parted for ever?
Where, through groves deep and high
   Sounds the far billow,
Where early violets die
   Under the willow.
     Eleu loro
Soft shall be his pillow.

There, through the summer day
  Cool streams are laving:
There, while the tempests sway,
  Scarce are boughs waving;
There thy rest shalt thou take,
  Parted for ever,
Never again to wake
  Never, O never!
    Eleu loro
  Never, O never!

Where shall the traitor rest,
  He, the deceiver,
Who could win maiden's breast,
  Ruin, and leave her?
In the lost battle,
  Borne down by the flying,
Where mingles war's rattle
  With groans of the dying;
    Eleu loro
  There shall he be lying.

Her wing shall the eagle flap
  O'er the falsehearted;
His warm blood the wolf shall lap
  Ere life be parted:
Shame and dishonour sit
  By his grave ever;
Blessing shall hallow it
  Never, O never!
    Eleu loro
  Never, O never!

                    Sir Walter Scott.

LIGHT O' LOVE.

"A WEARY lot is thine, fair maid,
　　A weary lot is thine!
To pull the thorn thy brow to braid,
　　And press the rue for wine!
A lightsome eye, a soldier's mien,
　　A feather of the blue,
A doublet of the Lincoln green,—
　　No more of me you knew,
　　　　　　　　My love!
　　No more of me you knew.

"This morn is merry June, I trow,
　　The rose is budding fain;
But she shall bloom in winter snow,
　　Ere we two meet again."
He turned his charger as he spake,
　　Upon the river shore,
He gave his bridle-reins a shake,
　　Said, "Adieu for evermore,
　　　　　　　　My love!
　　And adieu for evermore."

Sir W. Scott.

HIGHLAND MARY.

YE banks and braes and streams around
  The castle o' Montgomery,
Green be your woods, and fair your flowers,
  Your waters never drumlie!
There simmer first unfauld her robes,
  And there the langest tarry;
For there I took the last fareweel
  O' my sweet Highland Mary.

How sweetly bloom'd the gay green birk,
  How rich the hawthorn's blossom,
As underneath their fragrant shade
  I clasp'd her to my bosom!
The golden hours on angel wings
  Flew o'er me and my dearie;
For dear to me as light and life
  Was my sweet Highland Mary.

Wi' mony a vow and lock'd embrace
  Our parting was fu' tender;
And pledging aft to meet again,
  We tore oursels asunder;
But, O! fell Death's untimely frost,
  That nipt my flower sae early!
Now green's the sod, and cauld's the clay,
  That wraps my Highland Mary!

O pale, pale now, those rosy lips,
   I aft hae kiss'd sae fondly!
And closed for aye the sparkling glance
   That dwelt on me sae kindly;
And mouldering now in silent dust
   That heart that lo'ed me dearly!
But still within my bosom's core
   Shall live my Highland Mary.

                   R. Burns.

A WISH.

MINE be a cot beside the hill;
A bee-hive's hum shall soothe my ear;
A willowy brook that turns a mill,
With many a fall shall linger near.

The swallow, oft, beneath my thatch
Shall twitter from her clay-built nest;
Oft shall the pilgrim lift the latch,
And share my meal, a welcome guest.

Around my ivied porch shall spring
Each fragrant flower that drinks the dew;
And Lucy, at her wheel, shall sing
In russet-gown and apron blue.

The village-church among the trees,
Where first our marriage-vows were given,
With merry peals shall swell the breeze
And point with taper spire to Heaven.

                   Samuel Rogers.

LULLABY.

Sweet and low, sweet and low,
  Wind of the western sea,
Low, low, breathe and blow,
  Wind of the western sea!
Over the rolling waters go,
Come from the dying moon, and blow,
  Blow him again to me;
While my little one, while my pretty one, sleeps.

Sleep and rest, sleep and rest,
  Father will come to thee soon;
Rest, rest, on mother's breast,
  Father will come to thee soon;
Father will come to his babe in the nest,
Silver sails all out of the west
  Under the silver moon:
Sleep, my little one, sleep, my pretty one, sleep.

Alfred Tennyson.

THE PROMISE OF CHILDHOOD.

A ROSE-BUD by my early walk,
Adown a corn-enclosed bawk,
Sae gently bent its thorny stalk,
　All on a dewy morning.

Ere twice the shades o' dawn are fled,
In a' its crimson glory spread,
And drooping rich the dewy head,
　It scents the early morning.

Within the bush, her covert nest
A little linnet fondly prest,
The dew sat chilly on her breast
　Sae early in the morning.

She soon shall see her tender brood,
The pride, the pleasure o' the wood,
Amang the fresh green leaves bedew'd,
　Awake the early morning.

So thou, dear bird, young Jeany fair,
On trembling string, or vocal air,
Shall sweetly pay the tender care
　That tents thy early morning.

So thou, sweet rose-bud, young and gay,
Shalt beauteous blaze upon the day,
And bless the parent's evening ray
　That watch'd thy early morning.

R. Burns.

BLIGHTED IN THE BUD.

THREE years she grew in sun and shower;
Then Nature said, "A lovelier flower
On earth was never sown:
This child I to myself will take;
She shall be mine, and I will make
A lady of my own.

"Myself will to my darling be
Both law and impulse: and with me
The girl, in rock and plain,
In earth and heaven, in glade and bower
Shall feel an overseeing power
To kindle or restrain.

"She shall be sportive as the fawn
That wild with glee across the lawn
Or up the mountain springs;
And her's shall be the breathing balm,
And her's the silence and the calm
Of mute insensate things.

"The floating clouds their state shall lend
To her; for her the willow bend;
Nor shall she fail to see
E'en in the motions of the storm
Grace that shall mould the maiden's form
By silent sympathy.

"The stars of midnight shall be dear
  To her; and she shall lean her ear
  In many a secret place
  Where rivulets dance their wayward round,
  And beauty born of murmuring sound
  Shall pass into her face.

"And vital feelings of delight
  Shall rear her form to stately height,
  Her virgin bosom swell;
  Such thoughts to Lucy I will give
  While she and I together live
  Here in this happy dell."

Thus Nature spake.—The work was done—
  How soon my Lucy's race was run!
  She died, and left to me
  This heath, this calm and quiet scene;
  The memory of what has been,
  And never more will be.

William Wordsworth.

BEREAVEMENT.

SHE dwelt among the untrodden ways
　Beside the springs of Dove;
A maid whom there were none to praise,
　And very few to love.

A violet by a mossy stone
　Half-hidden from the eye!
—Fair as a star, when only one
　Is shining in the sky.

She lived unknown, and few could know
　When Lucy ceased to be;
But she is in her grave, and O!
　The difference to me!

W. Wordsworth.

RECONCILEMENT THROUGH LOSS.

As thro' the land at eve we went,
  And plucked the ripened ears,
We fell out, my wife and I,
We fell out, I know not why,
  And kissed again with tears.

And blessings on the falling out
  That all the more endears,
When we fall out with those we love,
  And kiss again with tears!

For when we came where lies the child
  We lost in other years,
There above the little grave,
O there above the little grave,
  We kissed again with tears.

A. Tennyson.

THE PAST.

WILT thou forget the happy hours
Which we buried in Love's sweet bowers,
Heaping over their corpses cold
Blossoms and leaves instead of mould?
Blossoms which were the joys that fell,
    And leaves, the hopes that yet remain.

Forget the dead, the past? Oh yet
There are ghosts that may take revenge for it!
Memories that make the heart a tomb,
Regrets which glide through the spirit's gloom,
And with ghastly whispers tell
    That joy, once lost, is pain.

Percy Bysshe Shelley.

NIGHT AND DEATH.

MYSTERIOUS Night! when our first parent knew
   Thee from report divine, and heard thy name,
Did he not tremble for this lovely frame,
   This glorious canopy of light and blue?
Yet 'neath a curtain of translucent dew,
   Bathed in the rays of the great setting flame,
Hesperus with the host of heaven came,
   And lo! creation widened in man's view.
Who could have thought such darkness lay concealed
   Within thy beams, O sun! or who could find,
Whilst fly, and leaf, and insect stood revealed,
   That to such countless orbs thou mad'st us blind!
Why do we then shun Death with anxious strife?
If light can thus deceive, wherefore not life?

J. Blanco White.

LONDON AT SUNRISE:

(FROM WESTMINSTER BRIDGE).

EARTH has not anything to show more fair:
Dull would he be of soul who could pass by
A sight so touching in its majesty:
This city now doth like a garment wear
The beauty of the morning; silent, bare,
Ships, towers, domes, theatres, and temples lie
Open unto the fields and to the sky,
All bright and glittering in the smokeless air.
Never did sun more beautifully steep
In his first splendour valley, rock, or hill;
Ne'er saw I, never felt, a calm so deep!
The river glideth at his own sweet will:
Dear God! the very houses seem asleep;
And all that mighty heart is lying still!

W. Wordsworth.

THE IDEAL HERMITAGE.

METHINKS that to some vacant hermitage
My feet would gladly turn—to some dry nook
Scooped out of living rock, and near a brook
Hurled down a mountain cove from stage to stage,
Yet tempering, for my sight, its bustling rage
In the soft heaven of a translucent pool;
Thence creeping under sylvan arches cool,
Fit haunt of shapes whose glorious equipage
Would elevate my dreams.   A beechen bowl,
A maple dish, my furniture should be;
Crisp, yellow leaves my bed; the hooting owl
My night-watch: nor should e'er the crested fowl
From thorp or vill his matins sound for me,
Tired of the world and all its industry.

W. Wordsworth.

RETIREMENT.

GIVE me a cottage on some Cambrian wild
Where, far from cities, I may spend my days,
And by the beauties of the scene beguil'd,
May pity man's pursuits, and shun his ways.
While on the rock I mark the browsing goat,
List to the mountain-torrent's distant noise,
Or the hoarse bittern's solitary note,
I shall not want the world's delusive joys;
But with my little scrip, my book, my lyre,
Shall think my lot complete, nor covet more;
And when, with time, shall wane the vital fire,
I'll raise my pillow on the desert shore,
And lay me down to rest where the wild wave
Shall make sweet music o'er my lonely grave.

Henry Kirke White.

FOR A GROTTO.

TO me, whom in their lays the shepherds call
Actæa, daughter of the neighbouring stream,
This cave belongs.   The fig-tree and the vine,
Which o'er the rocky entrance downward shoot,
Were placed by Glycon.   He with cowslips pale,
Primrose, and purple lychnis, decked the green
Before my threshold, and my shelving walls
With honeysuckle covered.   Here at noon,
Lulled by the murmur of my rising fount,
I slumber.   Here my clust'ring fruits I tend;
Or from my humid flow'rs at break of day
Fresh garlands weave; and chase from all my bounds
Each thing impure and noxious.   Enter in,
O stranger! undismayed.   Nor bat, nor toad
Here lurks; and if thy breast of blameless thought
Approve thee, not unwelcome shalt thou tread
My quiet mansion:—chiefly if thy name
Wise Pallas and the immortal Muses own.

Mark Akenside.

ODE TO CONTEMPLATION.

COME, pensive Sage, who lov'st to dwell
In some retired Lapponian cell,
Where far from noise and riot rude,
Resides sequestered solitude.
Come, and o'er my longing soul
Throw thy dark and russet stole,
And open to my duteous eyes
The volume of thy mysteries.

I will meet thee on the hill
Where, with printless footstep still,
The morning in her buskin grey
Springs upon her eastern way;
While the frolic zephyrs stir,
Playing with the gossamer,
And, on ruder pinions borne,
Shake the dew-drops from the thorn.
There, as o'er the fields we pass,
Brushing with hasty feet the grass,
We will startle from her nest
The lively lark with speckled breast,
And hear the floating clouds among
Her gale-transported matin song;
Or on the upland stile, embowered
With fragrant hawthorn snowy-flowered,
Will sauntering sit, and listen still,
To the herdsman's oaten quill

Wafted from the plain below;
Or the heifer's frequent low;
Or the milkmaid in the grove,
Singing of one that died for love.
  Or when the noontide heats oppress,
We will seek the dark recess
Where, in the embowered translucent stream,
The cattle shun the sultry beam;
And o'er us, on the marge reclined,
The drowsy fly her horn shall wind,
While echo, from her ancient oak,
Shall answer to the woodman's stroke;
Or the little peasant's song,
Wandering lone the glens among,
His artless lip with berries dyed,
And feet through ragged shoes descried.

But, oh, when evening's virgin Queen
Sits on her fringed throne serene,
We will seek the woody lane,
By the hamlet on the plain,
Where the weary rustic nigh
Shall whistle his wild melody,
And the croaking wicket oft
Shall echo from the neighbouring croft;
Or else, serenely silent, sit
By the brawling rivulet,
Which on its calm unruffled breast
Rears the old mossy arch impressed
That clasps its secret stream of glass,
Half hid in shrubs and waving grass,
The wood-nymph's lone secure retreat,
Unpressed by faun or sylvan's feet;
We'll watch in Eve's ethereal braid
The rich vermilion slowly fade;
Or catch, faint twinkling from afar,
The first glimpse of the eastern star.

And haply, then, with sudden swell,
Shall roar the distant curfew bell,
While in the castle's mouldering tower
The hooting owl is heard to pour
Her melancholy song, and scare
Dull silence brooding in the air.
Then, hermit, let us turn our feet
To the lone Abbey's still retreat,
Embowered in the distant glen,
Far from the busy haunts of men,
Where, as we sit upon the tomb,
The glow-worm's light may gild the gloom,
And show to Fancy's saddest eye
Where some lost hero's ashes lie.
And oh, as through the mouldering arch,
With ivy filled and weeping larch,
The night-gale whispers sadly clear,
Speaking dear things to fancy's ear,
We'll hold communion with the shade
Of some deep-wailing ruined maid—
Or call the ghost of Spenser down,
To tell of woe and fortune's frown;
And bid us cast the eye of hope,
Beyond this bad world's narrow scope.

Or if these joys to us denied,
To linger by the forest's side,
Or in the meadow or the wood,
Or by the lone romantic flood,
Let us in the busy town,
When sleep's dull streams the people drown,
Far from drowsy pillows flee,
And turn the church's massy key;
Then, as through the painted glass
The moon's pale beams obscurely pass,
And darkly on the trophied wall
Her faint ambiguous shadows fall,

Let us, while the faint winds wail
Through the long reluctant aisle,
As we pace with reverence meet,
Count the echoings of our feet,
While from the tombs, with confessed breath,
Distinct responds the voice of death.

If thou, mild Sage, wilt condescend
Thus on my footsteps to attend,
To thee my lonely lamp shall burn
By fallen Genius' sainted urn!
As o'er the scroll of Time I pore,
And sagely spell of ancient lore,
Till I can rightly guess of all
That Plato could to memory call;
And scan the formless views of things;
Or, with old Egypt's fettered kings,
Arrange the mystic trains that shine
In night's high philosophic mine;
And to thy name shall e'er belong
The honours of undying song.

H. K. White.

KUBLA KHAN:

A FRAGMENT.

In Xanadu did Kubla Khan
A stately pleasure-dome decree:
Where Alph, the sacred river, ran
Through caverns measureless to man
    Down to a sunless sea.
So twice five miles of fertile ground
With walls and towers were girdled round:
And there were gardens bright with sinuous rills
Where blossomed many an incense-bearing tree;
And here were forests ancient as the hills,
Enfolding sunny spots of greenery.

But oh! that deep romantic chasm which slanted
Down the green hill athwart a cedarn cover!
A savage place! as holy and enchanted
As e'er beneath a waning moon was haunted
By woman wailing for her demon-lover!
And from this chasm, with ceaseless turmoil seething,
As if this earth in fast thick pants were breathing,
A mighty fountain momently was forced;
Amid whose swift half-intermitted burst
Huge fragments vaulted like rebounding hail,
Or chaffy grain beneath the thresher's flail:
And 'mid these dancing rocks at once and ever
It flung up momently the sacred river.
Five miles meandering with a mazy motion
Through wood and dale the sacred river ran,

Then reached the caverns measureless to man,
And sank in tumult to a lifeless ocean:
And 'mid this tumult Kubla heard from far
Ancestral voices prophesying war!

    The shadow of the dome of pleasure
    Floated midway on the waves;
    Where was heard the mingled measure
    From the fountain and the caves.
It was a miracle of rare device,
A sunny pleasure-dome with caves of ice!
    A damsel with a dulcimer
    In a vision once I saw:
    It was an Abyssinian maid,
    And on her dulcimer she played,
    Singing of Mount Abora.
    Could I revive within me
    Her symphony and song,
    To such a deep delight 'twould win me
That with music loud and long,
I would build that dome in air,
That sunny dome! those caves of ice!
And all who heard should see them there,
And all should cry, Beware! Beware!
His flashing eyes, his floating hair!
Weave a circle round him thrice,
And close your eyes with holy dread,
For he on honey-dew hath fed,
And drunk the milk of Paradise.

Samuel Taylor Coleridge.

THE ISLES OF GREECE.

THE isles of Greece, the isles of Greece!
　Where burning Sappho loved and sung,
Where grew the arts of war and peace,—
　Where Delos rose, and Phœbus sprung!
Eternal summer gilds them yet,
But all, except their sun, is set.

The Scian and the Teian muse,
　The hero's harp, the lover's lute,
Have found the fame your shores refuse;
　Their place of birth alone is mute
To sounds which echo further west
Than your sires' "Islands of the Blest."

The mountains look on Marathon—
　And Marathon looks on the sea;
And musing there an hour alone,
　I dreamed that Greece might still be free;
For standing on the Persians' grave,
I could not deem myself a slave.

A king sat on the rocky brow
　Which looks o'er sea-born Salamis;
And ships by thousands lay below,
　And men in nations;—all were his!
He counted them at break of day—
And when the sun set, where were they?

And where are they? and where art thou,
  My country? On thy voiceless shore
The heroic lay is tuneless now—
  The heroic bosom beats no more!
And must thy lyre, so long divine,
Degenerate into hands like mine?

'Tis something, in the dearth of fame,
  Though linked among a fettered race,
To feel at least a patriot's shame,
  Even as I sing, suffuse my face;
For what is left the poet here?
For Greeks a blush—for Greece a tear.

Must we but weep o'er days more blest?
  Must we but blush?—Our fathers bled.
Earth! render back from out thy breast
  A remnant of our Spartan dead!
Of the three hundred grant but three,
To make a new Thermopylæ!

What, silent still? and silent all?
  Ah! no;—the voices of the dead
Sound like a distant torrent's fall,
  And answer, "Let one living head,
But one arise,—we come, we come!"
'Tis but the living who are dumb.

In vain—in vain; strike other chords;
  Fill high the cup with Samian wine!
Leave battles to the Turkish hordes,
  And shed the blood of Scio's vine!
Hark! rising to the ignoble call,
How answers each bold Bacchanal!

You have the Pyrrhic dance as yet—
   Where is the Pyrrhic phalanx gone?
Of two such lessons, why forget
   The nobler and the manlier one?
You have the letters Cadmus gave—
Think ye he meant them for a slave?

Fill high the bowl with Samian wine!
   We will not think of themes like these!
It made Anacreon's song divine:
   He served—but served Polycrates—
A tyrant; but our masters then
Were still, at least, our countrymen.

The tyrant of the Chersonese
   Was freedom's best and bravest friend;
That tyrant was Miltiades!
   Oh! that the present hour would lend
Another despot of the kind!
Such chains as his were sure to bind.

Fill high the bowl with Samian wine!
   On Suli's rock, and Parga's shore,
Exists the remnant of a line
   Such as the Doric mothers bore;
And there, perhaps, some seed is sown,
The Heracleidan blood might own.

Trust not for freedom to the Franks—
   They have a king who buys and sells:
In native swords, and native ranks,
   The only hope of courage dwells;
But Turkish force and Latin fraud
Would break your shield, however broad.

Fill high the bowl with Samian wine!
  Our virgins dance beneath the shade—
I see their glorious black eyes shine;
  But gazing on each glowing maid,
My own the burning tear-drop laves,
To think such breasts must suckle slaves.

Place me on Sunium's marbled steep,
  Where nothing, save the waves and I,
May hear our mutual murmurs sweep;
  There, swan-like, let me sing and die.
A land of slaves shall ne'er be mine—
Dash down yon cup of Samian wine!

Lord Byron.

EXURGAT HELLAS.

THE world's great age begins anew,
  The golden years return,
The earth doth like a snake renew
  Her winter weeds outworn:
Heaven smiles, and faiths and empires gleam
Like wrecks of a dissolving dream.

A brighter Hellas rears its mountains
  From waves serener far;
A new Peneus rolls his fountains
  Against the morning star;
Where fairer Tempes bloom, there sleep
Young Cyclads on a sunnier deep.

A loftier Argo cleaves the main,
  Fraught with a later prize;
Another Orpheus sings again,
  And loves, and weeps, and dies;
A new Ulysses leaves once more
Calypso for his native shore.

Oh! write no more the tale of Troy,
  If earth death's scroll must be—
Nor mix with Laian rage the joy
  Which dawns upon the free,
Although a subtler Sphinx renew
Riddles of death Thebes never knew.

Another Athens shall arise,
   And to remoter time
Bequeath, like sunset to the skies,
   The splendour of its prime;
And leave, if nought so bright may live,
All earth can take or heaven can give.

Saturn and Love their long repose
   Shall burst, more bright and good
Than all who fell, than one who rose,
   Than many unsubdued:
Not gold, not blood, their altar dowers,
But votive tears and symbol flowers.

Oh cease! must hate and death return?
   Cease! must men kill and die?
Cease! drain not to its dregs the urn
   Of bitter prophecy!
The world is weary of the past,—
Oh might it die or rest at last!

P. B. Shelley.

THE BOWL OF LIBERTY.

(FOR MODERN GREECE).

BEFORE the fiery sun,
The sun that looks on Greece with cloudless eye,
In the free air, and on the war-field won,
Our fathers crown'd the Bowl of Liberty.

Amidst the tombs they stood,
The tombs of heroes! with the solemn skies
And the wide plain around, where patriot-blood
Had steep'd the soil in hues of sacrifice.

They call'd the glorious dead,
In the strong faith which brings the viewless nigh,
And pour'd rich odours o'er the battle-bed,
And bade them to the rite of Liberty.

They call'd them from the shades,
The golden-fruited shades, where minstrels tell
How softer light th' immortal clíme pervades,
And music floats o'er meads of Asphodel.

Then fast the bright-red wine
Flow'd to *their* names who taught the world to die,
And made the land's green turf a living shrine,
Meet for the wreath and Bowl of Liberty.

3*

So the rejoicing earth
Took from her vines again the blood she gave,
And richer flowers to deck the tomb drew birth
From the free soil, thus hallow'd to the brave.

We have the battle-fields,
The tombs, the names, the blue majestic sky,
We have the founts the purple vintage yields;—
When shall *we* crown the Bowl of Liberty?

Mrs. Hemans.

THOUGHT, LIFE, AND DEATH.

HAST thou seen, with flash incessant,
Bubbles gliding under ice,
Bodied forth and evanescent,
No one knows by what device?

Such are Thoughts. A wind-swept meadow
Mimicking a troubled sea—
Such is Life; and Death, a shadow
From the rock, Eternity.

W. Wordsworth.

LIFE AND FAME.

THE flash at midnight!—'twas a light
That gave the blind a moment's sight,
　　Then sank in tenfold gloom;
Loud, deep, and long, the thunder broke,
The deaf ear instantly awoke,
　　Then closed as in the tomb:
An angel might have passed my bed,
Sounded the trump of God, and fled.

So life appears;—a sudden birth,
A glance revealing heaven and earth;
　　It *is*—and it is *not!*
So fame the poet's hope deceives,
Who sings for after time, and leaves
　　A name—to be forgot.
Life—is a lightning-flash of breath;
Fame—but a thunder-clap at death.

James Montgomery.

NEVERMORE.

O WORLD! O life! O time!
  On whose last steps I climb,
Trembling at that where I had stood before,—
When will return the glory of your prime?
  No more—Oh, never more!
  Out of the day and night
  A joy has taken flight:
Fresh spring, and summer, autumn, and winter hoar,
Move my faint heart with grief,—but with delight
  No more—Oh, never more!

P. B. Shelley.

SUSPIRIA.

TAKE them, O Death! and bear away
  Whatever thou canst call thine own!
Thine image, stamped upon this clay,
  Doth give thee that, but that alone!

Take them, O Grave! and let them lie
  Folded upon thy narrow shelves,
As garments by the soul laid by,
  And precious only to ourselves!

Take them, O great Eternity!
  Our little life is but a gust,
That bends the branches of thy tree,
  And trails its blossoms in the dust.

Henry Wadsworth Longfellow.

DEATH'S HARVEST-TIME.

LEAVES have their time to fall,
And flowers to wither at the north-wind's breath,
  And stars to set—but all,
Thou hast *all* seasons for thine own, O Death!

  Day is for mortal care;
Eve, for glad meetings round the joyous hearth;
  Night, for the dreams of sleep, the voice of prayer;—
But all for thee, thou Mightiest of the earth.

  The banquet hath its hour,
Its feverish hour, of mirth, and song, and wine;
  There comes a day for grief's o'erwhelming power,
A time for softer tears—but all are thine.

  Youth and the opening rose
May look like things too glorious for decay,
  And smile at thee—but thou art not of those
That wait the ripen'd bloom to seize their prey.

  Leaves have their time to fall,
And flowers to wither at the north-wind's breath,
  And stars to set—but all,
Thou hast *all* seasons for thine own, O Death!

  We know when moons shall wane,
When summer birds from far shall cross the sea,
  When autumn's hue shall tinge the golden grain—
But who shall teach us when to look for thee!

Is it when spring's first gale
Comes forth to whisper where the violets lie?
  Is it when roses in our paths grow pale?—
They have *one* season—*all* are ours to die!

    Thou art where billows foam,
Thou art where music melts upon the air;
  Thou art around us in our peaceful home,
And the world calls us forth—and thou art there.

    Thou art where friend meets friend,
Beneath the shadow of the elm to rest—
  Thou art where foe meets foe, and trumpets rend
The skies, and swords beat down the princely crest.

    Leaves have their time to fall,
And flowers to wither at the north-wind's breath,
  And stars to set—but all,
Thou hast *all* seasons for thine own, O Death!

Mrs. Hemans.

LOVE LEFT SORROWING.

'TIS said, that some have died for love:
And here and there a church-yard grave is found
In the cold north's unhallowed ground,
Because the wretched man himself had slain,
His love was such a grievous pain.
And there is one whom I five years have known;
He dwells alone
Upon Helvellyn's side:
He loved—the pretty Barbara died;
And thus he makes his moan:
Three years had Barbara in her grave been laid
When thus his moan he made:

"Oh, move, thou Cottage, from behind that oak!
Or let the aged tree uprooted lie,
That in some other way yon smoke
May mount into the sky!
The clouds pass on; they from the heavens depart:
I look—the sky is empty space;
I know not what I trace;
But when I cease to look, my hand is on my heart.

O! what a weight is in these shades! Ye leaves,
That murmur once so dear, when will it cease?
Your sound my heart of rest bereaves,
It robs my heart of peace.

Thou Thrush, that singest loud—and loud and free,
Into yon row of willows flit,
Upon that alder sit;
Or sing another song, or choose another tree.

Roll back, sweet Rill! back to thy mountain-bounds,
And there for ever be thy waters chained!
For thou dost haunt the air with sounds
That cannot be sustained;
If still beneath that pine-tree's ragged bough
Headlong yon waterfall must come,
Oh let it then be dumb!
Be anything, sweet Rill, but that which thou art now.

Thou Eglantine, so bright with sunny showers,
Proud as a rainbow spanning half the vale,
Thou one fair shrub, oh! shed thy flowers,
And stir not in the gale.
For thus to see thee nodding in the air,
To see thy arch thus stretch and bend,
Thus rise and thus descend,—
Disturbs me till the sight is more than I can bear."

The Man who makes this feverish complaint
Is one of giant stature, who could dance
Equipped from head to foot in iron mail.
Ah gentle Love! if ever thought was thine
To store up kindred hours for me, thy face
Turn from me, gentle Love! nor let me walk
Within the sound of Emma's voice, nor know
Such happiness as I have known to-day.

W. Wordsworth.

STANZAS

WRITTEN IN DEJECTION NEAR NAPLES.

THE sun is warm, the sky is clear,
   The waves are dancing fast and bright;
Blue isles and snowy mountains wear
    The purple noon's transparent might;
    The breath of the moist earth is light
Around its unexpanded buds;
    Like many a voice of one delight,
The winds', the birds', the ocean floods',
The city's voice itself, is soft like Solitude's.

I see the deep's untrampled floor
    With green and purple sea-weeds strown;
I see the waves upon the shore,
    Like light dissolved, in star-showers thrown.
    I sit upon the sands alone.
The lightning of the noontide ocean
    Is flashing round me, and a tone
Arises from its measured motion,—
How sweet, did any heart now share in my emotion!

Alas! I have nor hope nor health,
    Nor peace within nor calm around;
Nor that content, surpassing wealth,
    The sage in meditation found,

And walked with inward glory crowned;
Nor fame nor power nor love nor leisure.
  Others I see whom these surround—
Smiling they live, and call life pleasure;—
To me that cup has been dealt in another measure.

Yet now despair itself is mild,
  Even as the winds and waters are;
I could lie down like a tired child,
  And weep away the life of care
  Which I have borne and yet must bear,—
Till death like sleep might steal on me,
  And I might feel in the warm air
My cheek grow cold, and hear the sea
Breathe o'er my dying brain its last monotony.

Some might lament that I were cold,
  As I when this sweet day is gone,
Which my lost heart, too soon grown old,
  Insults with this untimely moan.
  They might lament—for I am one
Whom men love not, and yet regret;
  Unlike this day, which, when the sun
Shall on its stainless glory set,
Will linger, though enjoyed, like joy in memory yet.

                              P. B. Shelley.

LOCHINVAR.

O, YOUNG Lochinvar is come out of the west,
Through all the wide Border his steed was the best,
And save his good broad-sword he weapons had none;
He rode all unarmed, and he rode all alone.
So faithful in love, and so dauntless in war,
There never was knight like the young Lochinvar.

He stayed not for brake, and he stopped not for stone,
He swam the Eske river where ford there was none;
But, ere he alighted at Netherby gate,
The bride had consented, the gallant came late:
For a laggard in love, and a dastard in war,
Was to wed the fair Ellen of brave Lochinvar.

So boldly he entered the Netherby hall,
Among bride's-men and kinsmen, and brothers and all:
Then spoke the bride's father, his hand on his sword
(For the poor craven bridegroom said never a word),
"O come ye in peace here, or come ye in war,
Or to dance at our bridal, young Lord Lochinvar?"

"I long wooed your daughter, my suit you denied;—
Love swells like the Solway, but ebbs like its tide—
And now I am come, with this lost love of mine,
To lead but one measure, drink one cup of wine.
There are maidens in Scotland more lovely by far,
That would gladly be bride to the young Lochinvar."

The bride kissed the goblet; the knight took it up,
He quaffed off the wine, and he threw down the cup;
She looked down to blush, and she looked up to sigh,
With a smile on her lips and a tear in her eye.
He took her soft hand, ere her mother could bar,—
"Now tread we a measure!" said young Lochinvar.

So stately his form, and so lovely her face,
That never a hall such a galliard did grace;
While her mother did fret, and her father did fume,
And the bridegroom stood dangling his bonnet and plume;
And the bride-maidens whispered, "'Twere better by far
To have matched our fair cousin with young Lochinvar."

One touch to her hand, and one word in her ear,
When they reached the hall-door, and the charger stood
                near;
So light to the croupe the fair lady he swung,
So light to the saddle before her he sprung!
"She is won! we are gone, over bank, bush, and scaur;
They'll have fleet steeds that follow," quoth young Lochinvar.

There was mounting 'mong Græmes of the Netherby clan;
Forsters, Fenwicks, and Musgraves, they rode and they ran:
There was racing, and chasing, on Cannobie Lee,
But the lost bride of Netherby ne'er did they see.
So daring in love, and so dauntless in war,
Have ye e'er heard of gallant like young Lochinvar?

Sir W. Scott.

COME O'ER THE SEA.

COME o'er the sea,
Maiden, with me,
Mine through sunshine, storm, and snows;
Seasons may roll,
But the true soul
Burns the same, where'er it goes.
Let fate frown on, so we love and part not;
'Tis life where thou art, 'tis death where thou art not.
Then come o'er the sea,
Maiden, with me,
Come wherever the wild wind blows;
Seasons may roll,
But the true soul
Burns the same, where'er it goes.

Was not the sea
Made for the free,
Land for courts and chains alone?
Here we are slaves,
But on the waves
Love and liberty's all our own.
No eye to watch, and no tongue to wound us,
All earth forgot, and all heaven around us—
Then come o'er the sea,
Maiden, with me,
Mine through sunshine, storm, and snows;
Seasons may roll,
But the true soul
Burns the same, where'er it goes.

Thomas Moore.

JOCK O' HAZELDEAN.

"WHY weep ye by the tide, ladie?
    Why weep ye by the tide?
I'll wed ye to my youngest son,
    And ye sall be his bride:
And ye sall be his bride, ladie,
    Sae comely to be seen"—
But aye she loot the tears down fa'
    For Jock of Hazeldean.

"Now let this wilfu' grief be done,
    And dry that cheek so pale;
Young Frank is chief of Errington
    And lord of Langley-dale;
His step is first in peaceful ha',
    His sword in battle keen"—
But aye she loot the tears down fa'
    For Jock of Hazeldean.

"A chain of gold ye sall not lack,
    Nor braid to bind your hair,
Nor mettled hound, nor managed hawk,
    Nor palfrey fresh and fair;
And you the foremost o' them a'
    Shall ride our forest-queen"—
But aye she loot the tears down fa'
    For Jock of Hazeldean.

The kirk was deck'd at morning-tide,
   The tapers glimmer'd fair;
The priest and bridegroom wait the bride,
   And dame and knight are there:
They sought her baith by bower and ha';
   The ladie was not seen!
She's o'er the Border, and awa'
   Wi' Jock of Hazeldean.

Sir W. Scott.

THE YOUNG MAY MOON.

THE young May moon is beaming, love,
The glow-worm's lamp is gleaming, love,
     How sweet to rove
     Through Morna's grove,
When the drowsy world is dreaming, love!
Then awake!—the heavens look bright, my dear,
'Tis never too late for delight, my dear,
     And the best of all ways
     To lengthen our days
Is to steal a few hours from the night, my dear.

Now all the world is sleeping, love,
But the Sage, his star-watch keeping, love,
     And I whose star,
     More glorious far,
Is the eye from that casement peeping, love.
Then awake!—till rise of sun, my dear,
The Sage's glass we'll shun, my dear,
     Or, in watching the flight
     Of bodies of light,
He might happen to take thee for one, my dear.

T. Moore.

INSUFFICIENCY.

THERE is no one beside thee and no one above thee,
  Thou standest alone, as the nightingale sings!
  And my words that would praise thee are impotent things.
For none can express thee though all should approve thee.
  I love thee so, Dear, that I only can love thee.

Say what can I do for thee? weary thee, grieve thee?
  Lean on thy shoulder, new burdens to add?
  Weep my tears over thee, making thee sad?
Oh, hold me not—love me not! let me retrieve thee.
  I love thee so, Dear, that I only can leave thee.

Elizabeth Barrett Browning.

INCLUSIONS.

OH! wilt thou have my hand, Dear, to lie along in thine?
As a little stone in a running stream, it seems to lie and
    pine.
Now drop the poor pale hand, Dear, . . unfit to plight with
    thine.

Oh! wilt thou have my cheek, Dear, drawn closer to thine
    own?
My cheek is white, my cheek is worn, by many a tear run
    down.
Now leave a little space, Dear, . . lest it should wet thine
    own.

Oh! must thou have my soul, Dear, commingled with thy
    soul?
Red grows the cheek, and warm the hand, . . the part is in
    the whole!
Nor hands nor cheeks keep separate, when soul is joined to
    soul.

E. B. Browning.

LINES TO AN INDIAN AIR.

I ARISE from dreams of thee
  In the first sweet sleep of night,
When the winds are breathing low,
  And the stars are shining bright.
I arise from dreams of thee,
  And a spirit in my feet
Hath led me—who knows how?
  To thy chamber window, sweet!

The wandering airs they faint
  On the dark, the silent stream—
The champak odours fail
  Like sweet thoughts in a dream;
The nightingale's complaint
  It dies upon her heart,
As I must die on thine,
  Belovèd as thou art!

Oh lift me from the grass!
  I die, I faint, I fail!
Let thy love in kisses rain
  On my lips and eyelids pale.
My cheek is cold and white, alas!
  My heart beats loud and fast:
Oh! press it close to thine again,
  Where it will break at last.

P. B. Shelley.

A NIGHT-SONG OF LOVE.

Now sleeps the crimson petal, now the white;
Nor waves the cypress in the palace walk;
Nor winks the gold fin in the porphyry font:
The fire-fly wakens: waken thou with me.

Now droops the milkwhite peacock like a ghost,
And like a ghost she glimmers on to me.

Now lies the Earth all Danaë to the stars,
And all thy heart lies open unto me.

Now slides the silent meteor on, and leaves
A shining furrow, as thy thoughts in me.

Now folds the lily all her sweetness up,
And slips into the bosom of the lake:
So fold thyself, my dearest, thou, and slip
Into my bosom and be lost in me.

A. Tennyson.

MORNING SONG TO MAUD.

1.

Come into the garden, Maud,
  For the black bat, night, has flown,
Come into the garden, Maud,
  I am here at the gate alone;
And the woodbine spices are wafted abroad,
  And the musk of the roses blown.

2.

For a breeze of morning moves,
  And the planet of Love is on high,
Beginning to faint in the light that she loves
  On a bed of daffodil sky,
To faint in the light of the sun she loves,
  To faint in his light, and to die.

3.

There has fall'n a splendid tear
  From the passion-flower at the gate.
She is coming, my dove, my dear;
  She is coming, my life, my fate;
The red rose cries, "She is near, she is near;"
  And the white rose weeps, "She is late;"
The larkspur listens, "I hear, I hear;"
  And the lily whispers, "I wait."

4.

She is coming, my own, my sweet;
  Were it ever so airy a tread,
My heart would hear her and beat,
  Were it earth in an earthy bed;
My dust would hear her and beat
  Had I lain for a century dead;
Would start and tremble under her feet,
  And blossom in purple and red.

                                    A. Tennyson.

A FAREWELL.

Go fetch to me a pint o' wine,
    And fill it in a silver tassie;
That I may drink before I go
    A service to my bonnie lassie:
The boat rocks at the pier of Leith,
    Fu' loud the wind blaws frae the Ferry,
The ship rides by the Berwick-law,
    And I maun leave my bonnie Mary.

The trumpets sound, the banners fly,
    The glittering spears are rankéd ready;
The shouts o' war are heard afar,
    The battle closes thick and bloody:
But it's not the roar o' sea or shore
    Wad make me langer wish to tarry;
Nor shouts o' war that's heard afar—
    It's leaving thee, my bonnie Mary.

                                    R. Burns.

THE MINSTREL-BOY.

THE Minstrel-boy to the war is gone,
   In the ranks of death you'll find him;
His father's sword he has girded on,
   And his wild harp slung behind him.—
"Land of song!" said the warrior-bard,
   "Though all the world betrays thee,
One sword, at least, thy rights shall guard,
   One faithful harp shall praise thee!"

The Minstrel fell!—but the foeman's chain
   Could not bring his proud soul under;
The harp he loved ne'er spoke again,
   For he tore its chords asunder;
And said, "No chains shall sully thee,
   Thou soul of love and bravery!
Thy songs were made for the brave and free,
   They shall never sound in slavery!"

T. Moore.

BANNOCKBURN.

ROBERT BRUCE'S ADDRESS TO HIS ARMY.

SCOTS, wha hae wi' Wallace bled,
Scots, wham Bruce has aften led;
Welcome to your gory bed,
   Or to victory!

Now's the day, and now's the hour;
See the front o' battle lower:
See approach proud Edward's pow'r—
   Chains and slavery!

Wha will be a traitor knave?
Wha would fill a coward's grave?
Wha sae base as be a slave?
   Let him turn and flee!

Wha for Scotland's King and law
Freedom's sword will strongly draw,
Free-man stand, or free-man fa'?
   Let him on wi' me!

By Oppression's woes and pains,
By your sons in servile chains,
We will drain our dearest veins,
   But they shall be free!

Lay the proud usurpers low!
Tyrants fall in every foe!
Liberty's in every blow!
   Let us do, or die!

R. Burns.

LIBERTY OR DEATH.

OH, where's the slave so lowly
Condemned to chains unholy,
    Who, could he burst
    His bonds at first,
Would pine beneath them slowly?
What soul, whose wrongs degrade it,
Would wait till time decayed it,
    When thus its wing
    At once may spring
To the throne of Him who made it?
  Farewell, Erin,—farewell, all
  Who live to weep our fall.

Less dear the laurel growing
Alive, untouched, and blowing,
    Than that whose braid
    Is plucked to shade
The brows with victory glowing.
We tread the land that bore us,
Her green flag glitters o'er us,
    The friends we've tried
    Are by our side,
And the foe we hate before us.
  Farewell, Erin,—farewell, all
  Who live to weep our fall.

T. Moore.

THE BATTLE OF IVRY.

Now glory to the Lord of hosts, from whom all glories are!
And glory to our Sovereign Liege, King Henry of Navarre!
Now let there be the merry sound of music and of dance,
Through thy corn-fields green, and sunny vines, oh pleasant
　　　　land of France!
And thou, Rochelle, our own Rochelle, proud city of the
　　　　waters,
Again let rapture light the eyes of all thy mourning daughters.
As thou wert constant in our ills, be joyous in our joy,
For cold, and stiff, and still are they who wrought thy walls
　　　　annoy.
Hurrah! hurrah! a single field hath turned the chance of war,
Hurrah! hurrah! for Ivry, and King Henry of Navarre.

Oh! how our hearts were beating, when at the dawn of day
We saw the army of the League drawn out in long array;
With all its priest-led citizens, and all its rebel peers,
And Appenzel's stout infantry, and Egmont's Flemish spears.
There rode the brood of false Lorraine, the curses of our
　　　　land!
And dark Mayenne was in the midst, a truncheon in his
　　　　hand!
And as we looked on them, we thought of Seine's empurpled
　　　　flood,
And good Coligni's hoary hair all dabbled with his blood;
And we cried unto the living God, who rules the fate of war,
To fight for his own holy name, and Henry of Navarre.

The King is come to marshal us, in all his armour drest,
And he has bound a snow-white plume upon his gallant crest.
He looked upon his people, and a tear was in his eye;
He looked upon the traitors, and his glance was stern and
        high.
Right graciously he smiled on us, as rolled from wing to
        wing,
Down all our line, a deafening shout, "God save our Lord
        the King!"
"And if my standard-bearer fall, as fall full well he may,
For never saw I promise yet of such a bloody fray,
Press where ye see my white plume shine, amidst the ranks
        of war,
And be your oriflamme to-day the helmet of Navarre."

Hurrah! the foes are moving. Hark to the mingled din
Of fife, and steed, and trump and drum, and roaring culverin!
The fiery Duke is pricking fast across Saint André's plain,
With all the hireling chivalry of Guelders and Almayne.
Now by the lips of those ye love, fair gentlemen of France,
Charge for the Golden Lilies now—upon them with the lance!
A thousand spurs are striking deep, a thousand spears in
        rest,
A thousand knights are pressing close behind the snow-
        white crest;
And in they burst, and on they rushed, while, like a guiding
        star,
Amidst the thickest carnage blazed the helmet of Navarre.

Now, God be praised, the day is ours! Mayenne hath turned
        his rein.
D'Aumale hath cried for quarter. The Flemish Count is
        slain.
Their ranks are breaking like thin clouds before a Biscay
        gale;
The field is heaped with bleeding steeds, and flags, and
        cloven mail;

And then, we thought on vengeance, and, all along our van,
"Remember St. Bartholomew," was passed from man to
man;
But out spake gentle Henry, "No Frenchman is my foe:
Down, down with every foreigner, but let your brethren go."
Oh! was there ever such a knight, in friendship or in war,
As our Sovereign Lord King Henry, the soldier of Navarre!

Ho! maidens of Vienna! Ho! matrons of Lucerne!
Weep, weep, and rend your hair for those who never shall
return.
Ho! Philip, send, for charity, thy Mexican pistoles,
That Antwerp monks may sing a mass for thy poor spear-
men's souls!
Ho! gallant nobles of the League, look that your arms be
bright!
Ho! burghers of Saint Genevieve, keep watch and ward to-
night!
For our God hath crushed the tyrant, our God hath raised
the slave,
And mocked the counsel of the wise, and the valour of the
brave.
Then glory to His holy name, from whom all glories are;
And glory to our Sovereign Lord, King Henry of Navarre.

Lord Macaulay.

HOHENLINDEN.

On Linden when the sun was low,
All bloodless lay the untrodden snow;
And dark as winter was the flow
    Of Iser rolling rapidly.

But Linden saw another sight
When the drum beat at dead of night,
Commanding fires of death to light
    The darkness of her scenery.

By torch and trumpet fast arrayed,
Each horseman drew his battle blade,
And furious every charger neighed
    To join the dreadful revelry.

Then shook the hills, with thunder riven;
Then rushed the steed, to battle driven;
And louder than the bolts of Heaven
    Far flashed the red artillery.

But redder yet that light shall glow
On Linden's hills of stained snow,
And bloodier yet the torrent flow
    Of Iser rolling rapidly.

'Tis morn, but scarce yon level sun
Can pierce the war-clouds, rolling dun,
Where furious Frank and fiery Hun
    Shout in their sulph'rous canopy.

The combat deepens. On, ye brave,
Who rush to glory or the grave!
Wave, Munich, all thy banners wave,
 And charge with all thy chivalry.

Few, few shall part where many meet;
The snow shall be their winding-sheet;
And every turf beneath their feet
 Shall be a soldier's sepulchre.

      Thomas Campbell.

GATHERING SONG OF DONALD THE BLACK.

PIBROCH of Donuil Dhu,
 Pibroch of Donuil,
Wake thy wild voice anew,
 Summon Clan Conuil.
Come away, come away,
 Hark to the summons!
Come in your war-array,
 Gentles and commons.

Come from deep glen, and
 From mountain so rocky;
The war-pipe and pennon
 Are at Inverlocky.
Come every hill-plaid, and
 True heart that wears one,
Come every steel blade, and
 Strong hand that bears one.

Leave untended the herd,
  The flock without shelter;
Leave the corpse uninterr'd,
  The bride at the altar;
Leave the deer, leave the steer,
  Leave nets and barges:
Come with your fighting gear,
  Broadswords and targes.

Come as the winds come, when
  Forests are rended,
Come as the waves come, when
  Navies are stranded:
Faster come, faster come,
  Faster and faster,
Chief, vassal, page and groom,
  Tenant and master.

Fast they come, fast they come;
  See how they gather!
Wide waves the eagle plume
  Blended with heather.
Cast your plaids, draw your blades,
  Forward each man set!
Pibroch of Donuil Dhu
  Knell for the onset!

Sir W. Scott.

CORONACH.

He is gone on the mountain,
  He is lost to the forest,
Like a summer-dried fountain,
  When our need was the sorest.
The fount reappearing
  From the raindrops shall borrow,
But to us comes no cheering,
  To Duncan no morrow!

The hand of the reaper
  Takes the ears that are hoary,
But the voice of the weeper
  Wails manhood in glory.
The autumn winds rushing
  Waft the leaves that are serest,
But our flower was in flushing
  When blighting was nearest.

Fleet foot on the correi,
  Sage counsel in cumber,
Red hand in the foray,
  How sound is thy slumber!
Like the dew on the mountain,
  Like the foam on the river,
Like the bubble on the fountain,
  Thou art gone; and for ever!—

Sir W. Scott.

THE BURIAL OF SIR JOHN MOORE.

NOT a drum was heard, not a funeral note,
  As his corse to the rampart we hurried;
Not a soldier discharged his farewell shot
  O'er the grave where our hero we buried.

We buried him darkly at dead of night,
  The sods with our bayonets turning;
By the struggling moonbeam's misty light,
  And the lantern dimly burning.

No useless coffin enclosed his breast,
  Not in sheet nor in shroud we wound him;
But he lay like a warrior taking his rest,
  With his martial cloak around him.

Few and short were the prayers we said,
  And we spoke not a word of sorrow;
But we steadfastly gazed on the face that was dead,
  And we bitterly thought of the morrow.

We thought, as we hollow'd his narrow bed
  And smoothed down his lonely pillow,
That the foe and the stranger would tread o'er his hea
  And we far away on the billow!

Lightly they'll talk of the spirit that's gone
 And o'er his cold ashes upbraid him,—
But little he'll reck, if they let him sleep on
 In the grave where a Briton has laid him.

But half of our heavy task was done
 When the clock struck the hour for retiring;
And we heard the distant and random gun
 That the foe was sullenly firing.

Slowly and sadly we laid him down,
 From the field of his fame fresh and gory;
We carved not a line, and we raised not a stone—
 But we left him alone with his glory.

Charles Wolfe.

ENGLAND'S DEAD.

SON of the ocean isle!
 Where sleep your mighty dead?
Show me what high and stately pile
 Is rear'd o'er Glory's bed.

Go, stranger! track the deep,
 Free, free, the white sail spread!
Wave may not foam, nor wild wind sweep,
 Where rest not England's dead.

On Egypt's burning plains,
 By the pyramid o'ersway'd,
With fearful power the noon-day reigns,
 And the palm-trees yield no shade.

5*

But let the angry sun
From Heaven look fiercely **red**,
Unfelt by those whose task is **done!**
  There slumber England's **dead.**

The hurricane hath might
Along the Indian shore,
And far, by Ganges' banks at **night,**
  Is heard the tiger's **roar.**

But let the sound roll on!
It hath no tone of dread,
For those that from their toils **are gone;—**
  There slumber England's **dead!**

Loud rush the torrent-**floods**
The western wilds among,
And free, in green Columbia's **woods,**
  The hunter's bow is strung.

But let the floods rush on!
Let the arrow's flight be sped!
Why should *they* reck whose task is **done?**
  There slumber England's **dead!**

The mountain-storms rise high
In the snowy Pyrenees,
And toss the pine-boughs through **the sky,**
  Like rose-leaves on the breeze.

But let the storm rage on!
Let the forest-wreaths be shed;
For the Roncesvalles' field is won,—
  There slumber England's dead.

On the frozen deep's repose
'Tis a dark and dreadful hour,
When round the ship the ice-fields close,
To chain her with their power.

But let the ice drift on!
Let the cold-blue desert spread!
Their course with mast and flag is done,
There slumber England's dead.

The warlike of the isles,
The men of field and wave!
Are not the rocks their funeral piles,
The seas and shores their grave?

Go, stranger! track the deep,
Free, free the white sail spread!
Wave may not foam, nor wild wind sweep,
Where rest not England's dead.

Mrs. Hemans.

AFTER BLENHEIM.

IT was a summer evening,
  Old Kaspar's work was done,
And he before his cottage door
  Was sitting in the sun;
And by him sported on the green
His little grandchild Wilhelmine.

She saw her brother Peterkin
  Roll something large and round
Which he beside the rivulet
  In playing there had found;
He came to ask what he had found
That was so large and smooth and round.

Old Kaspar took it from the boy
  Who stood expectant by:
And then the old man shook his head,
  And with a natural sigh
"'Tis some poor fellow's skull," said he,
"Who fell in the great victory.

"I find them in the garden,
  For there's many here about;
And often when I go to plough
  The ploughshare turns them out.
For many thousand men," said he,
"Were slain in that great victory."

"Now tell us what 'twas all about,"
    Young Peterkin he cries;
  And little Wilhelmine looks up
    With wonder-waiting eyes;
"Now tell us all about the war,
  And what they fought each other for."

"It was the English," Kaspar cried,
    "Who put the French to rout;
  But what they fought each other for
    I could not well make out.
  But every body said," quoth he, ·
"That 'twas a famous victory.

"My father lived at Blenheim then,
    Yon little stream hard by;
  They burnt his dwelling to the ground,
    And he was forced to fly:
  So with his wife and child he fled,
  Nor had he where to rest his head.

"With fire and sword the country round
    Was wasted far and wide,
  And many a childing mother then
    And newborn baby died:
  But things like that, you know, must be
  At every famous victory.

"They say it was a shocking sight
    After the field was won;
  For many thousand bodies here
    Lay rotting in the sun:
  But things like that, you know, must be
  After a famous victory.

"Great praise the Duke of Marlbro' won,
    And our good Prince Eugene;"
"Why 'twas a very wicked thing!"
    Said little Wilhelmine;
"Nay .. nay .. my little girl," quoth he,
"It was a famous victory.

"And everybody praised the Duke
    Who this great fight did win."
"But what good came of it at last?"
    Quoth little Peterkin:—
"Why that I cannot tell," said he,
"But 'twas a famous victory."

Robert Southey.

OZYMANDIAS OF EGYPT.

I MET a traveller from an antique land
Who said: Two vast and trunkless legs of stone
Stand in the desert. Near them on the sand,
Half sunk, a shatter'd visage lies, whose frown
And wrinkled lip and sneer of cold command
Tell that its sculptor well those passions read
Which yet survive, stamp'd on these lifeless things,
The hand that mock'd them and the heart that fed;
And on the pedestal these words appear:
"My name is Ozymandias, king of kings:
Look on my works, ye Mighty, and despair!"
Nothing beside remains. Round the decay
Of that colossal wreck, boundless and bare,
The lone and level sands stretch far away.

P. B. Shelley.

THE NILE.

IT flows through old hushed Egypt and its sands,
  Like some grave mighty thought threading a dream;
  And times and things, as in that vision, seem
  Keeping along it their eternal stands,—
Caves, pillars, pyramids, the shepherd bands
  That roamed through the young world, the glory extreme
  Of high Sesostris, and that southern beam,
  The laughing queen that caught the world's great hands.
Then comes a mightier silence, stern and strong,
  As of a world left empty of its throng,
  And the void weighs on us; and then we wake,
And hear the fruitful stream lapsing along
  'Twixt villages, and think how we shall take
  Our own calm journey on for human sake.

Leigh Hunt.

EGYPT.

FANTASTIC sleep is busy with my eyes:
  I seem in some waste solitude to stand
  Once ruled of Cheops: upon either hand
A dark, illimitable desert lies,
Sultry and still—a realm of mysteries;
  A wide-browed Sphinx, half buried in the sand,
  With orbless sockets stares across the land,
The wofullest thing beneath these brooding skies
Where all is woful weird-lit vacancy.
  'Tis neither midnight, twilight, nor moonrise.
Lo! while I gaze, beyond the vast sand-sea
  The nebulous clouds are downward slowly drawn,
And one blear'd star, faint-glimmering like a bee,
  Is shut i' the rosy outstretched hand of Dawn.

Thomas Bailey Aldrich.

ROMAN ANTIQUITIES DISCOVERED.

WHILE poring Antiquarians search the ground
Upturned with curious pains, the bard, a Seer,
Takes fire:—the men that have been reappear;
Romans for travel girt, for business gowned;
And some recline on couches, myrtle-crowned,
In festal glee.   Why not? For fresh and clear,
As if its hues were of the passing year,
Dawns this time-buried pavement.   From that mound
Hoards may come forth of Trajans, Maximins,
Shrunk into coins with all their warlike toil:
Or a fierce impress issue with its foil
Of tenderness—the Wolf, whose suckling Twins
The unlettered ploughboy pities, when he wins
The casual treasure from the furrow'd soil.

W. Wordsworth.

ON FIRST LOOKING INTO CHAPMAN'S HOMER.

MUCH have I travell'd in the realms of gold
And many goodly states and kingdoms seen;
Round many western islands have I been
Which bards in fealty to Apollo hold.

Oft of one wide expanse had I been told
That deep-brow'd Homer ruled as his demesne:
Yet did I never breathe its pure serene
Till I heard Chapman speak out loud and bold:

—Then felt I like some watcher of the skies
When a new planet swims into his ken;
Or like stout Cortez—when with eagle eyes

He stared at the Pacific, and all his men
Look'd at each other with a wild surmise—
Silent, upon a peak in Darien.

John Keats.

FANCY IN NUBIBUS.

OR THE POET IN THE CLOUDS.

O! IT is pleasant, with a heart at ease,
  Just after sunset, or by moonlight skies,
To make the shifting clouds be what you please,
  Or let the easily persuaded eyes
Own each quaint likeness issuing from the mould
  Of a friend's fancy; or, with head bent low
And cheek aslant, see rivers flow of gold
  'Twixt crimson banks; and then, a traveller, go
From mount to mount through Cloudland, gorgeous land!
  Or list'ning to the tide, with closèd sight,
Be that blind bard who, on the Chian strand
  By those deep sounds possessed with inward light,
Beheld the Iliad and the Odyssee
Rise to the swelling of the voiceful sea.

S. T. Coleridge.

WITH A COPY OF THE ILIAD.

BAYARD, awaken not this music strong
While round thy home the indolent sweet breeze
Floats lightly as the summer breath of seas
O'er which Ulysses heard the Siren's song!
Dreams of low-lying isles to June belong,
And Circe holds us in her haunts of ease;
But later, when these high ancestral trees
Are sear, and such Odyssean languors wrong
The reddening strength of the autumnal year,
Yield to heroic words thine ear and eye:
Intent on these broad pages thou shalt hear
The trumpet's blare, the Argive battle-cry,
And see Achilles hurl his hurtling spear,
And mark the Trojan arrows make reply.

Edmund Clarence Stedman.

TO MILTON.

MILTON! thou shouldst be living at this hour;
England hath need of thee: she is a fen
Of stagnant waters: altar, sword, and pen,
Fireside, the heroic wealth of hall and bower,
Have forfeited their ancient English dower
Of inward happiness.   We are selfish men:
Oh! raise us up, return to us again;
And give us manners, virtue, freedom, power.
Thy soul was like a star, and dwelt apart:
Thou hadst a voice whose sound was like the sea;
Pure as the naked heavens, majestic, free;
So didst thou travel on life's common way,
In cheerful godliness; and yet thy heart
The lowliest duties on itself did lay.

W. Wordsworth.

THE MEMORY OF GREAT POETS.

WRITTEN IN A VOLUME OF SHAKESPEARE.

How bravely Autumn paints upon the sky
The gorgeous fame of Summer which is fled!
Hues of all flow'rs, that in their ashes lie,
Trophied in that fair light whereon they fed,—
Tulip, and hyacinth, and sweet rose red,—
Like exhalations from the leafy mould,
Look here how honour glorifies the dead,
And warms their scutcheons with a glance of gold!—
Such is the memory of poets old,
Who on Parnassus-hill have bloom'd elate;
Now they are laid under their marbles cold,
And turn'd to clay, whereof they were create;
But god Apollo hath them all enroll'd,
And blazon'd on the very clouds of Fate!

Thomas Hood.

THE WORLD OF BOOKS.

WINGS have we—and as far as we can go,
We may find pleasure: wilderness and wood,
Blank ocean and mere sky, support that mood
Which, with the lofty, sanctifies the low;
Dreams, books, are each a world; and books, we know,
Are a substantial world, both pure and good:
Round these, with tendrils strong as flesh and blood,
Our pastime and our happiness will grow.
There do I find a never-failing store
Of personal themes, and such as I love best;
Matter wherein right voluble I am;
Two will I mention, dearer than the rest:
The gentle lady married to the Moor;
And heavenly Una, with her milk-white lamb.

W. Wordsworth.

THE SCHOLAR IN HIS LIBRARY.

My days among the Dead are pass'd;
    Around me I behold,
Where'er these casual eyes are cast,
    The mighty minds of old;
My never-failing friends are they
With whom I converse night and day.

With them I take delight in weal,
    And seek relief in woe;
And while I understand and feel
    How much to them I owe,
My cheeks have often been bedew'd
With tears of thoughtful gratitude.

My thoughts are with the Dead: with them
    I live in long past years,
Their virtues love, their faults condemn,
    Partake their griefs and fears;
And from their sober lessons find
Instruction with a humble mind.

My hopes are with the Dead: anon
    With them my place will be;
And I with them shall travel on
    Through all futurity;
Yet leaving here a name, I trust,
Which will not perish in the dust.

R. Southey.

ODE TO THE WEST WIND.

O WILD West Wind, thou breath of Autumn's being,
Thou, from whose unseen presence the leaves dead
Are driven, like ghosts from an enchanter fleeing,
Yellow, and black, and pale, and hectic red,
Pestilence-stricken multitudes: O thou
Who chariotest to their dark wintry bed
The wingéd seeds, where they lie cold and low,
Each like a corpse within its grave, until
Thine azure sister of the spring shall blow
Her clarion o'er the dreaming earth, and fill
(Driving sweet buds like flocks to feed in air)
With living hues and odours plain and hill:
Wild Spirit, which art moving everywhere;
Destroyer and Preserver; Hear, O hear!

Thou on whose stream, 'mid the steep sky's commotion,
Loose clouds like earth's decaying leaves are shed
Shook from the tangled boughs of Heaven and Ocean,
Angels of rain and lightning; there are spread
On the blue surface of thine airy surge,
Like the bright hair uplifted from the head
Of some fierce Mænad, ev'n from the dim verge
Of the horizon to the zenith's height—
The locks of the approaching storm. Thou dirge
Of the dying year, to which this closing night
Will be the dome of a vast sepulchre,
Vaulted with all thy congregated might
Of vapours, from whose solid atmosphere
Black rain, and fire, and hail, will burst: O hear!

Thou who didst waken from his summer-dreams
The blue Mediterranean, where he lay
Lull'd by the coil of his crystalline streams
Beside a pumice isle in Baiæ's bay,
And saw in sleep old palaces and towers
Quivering within the wave's intenser-day,
All overgrown with azure moss and flowers
So sweet, the sense faints picturing them! Thou
For whose path the Atlantic's level powers
Cleave themselves into chasms, while, far below,
The sea-blooms and the oozy woods which wear
The sapless foliage of the ocean, know
Thy voice, and suddenly grow gray with fear
And tremble and despoil themselves: O hear!

If I were a dead leaf thou mightest bear;
If I were a swift cloud to fly with thee;
A wave to pant beneath thy power, and share
The impulse of thy strength, only less free
Than Thou, O uncontrollable! If even
I were as in my boyhood, and could be
The comrade of thy wanderings over heaven,
As then, when to outstrip the skyey speed
Scarce seem'd a vision, I would ne'er have striven
As thus with thee in prayer in my sore need.
O lift me as a wave, a leaf, a cloud!
I fall upon the thorns of life! I bleed!
A heavy weight of hours has chain'd and bow'd
One too like thee: tameless, and swift, and proud.

Make me thy lyre, ev'n as the forest is:
What if my leaves are falling like its own!
The tumult of thy mighty harmonies
Will take from both a deep autumnal tone,
Sweet though in sadness. Be thou, Spirit fierce,
My spirit! be thou me, impetuous one!
Drive my dead thoughts over the universe

Like wither'd leaves to quicken a new birth;
And, by the incantation of this verse,
Scatter, as from an unextinguish'd hearth
Ashes and sparks, my words among mankind!
Be through my lips to unawaken'd earth
The trumpet of a prophecy! O Wind,
If Winter comes, can Spring be far behind?

P. B. Shelley.

ODE TO AUTUMN.

SEASON of mists and mellow fruitfulness!
Close bosom-friend of the maturing sun;
Conspiring with him how to load and bless
With fruit the vines that round the thatch-eaves run:
To bend with apples the moss'd cottage-trees,
And fill all fruit with ripeness to the core;
To swell the gourd, and plump the hazel shells
With a sweet kernel; to set budding more
And still more, later flowers for the bees,
Until they think warm days will never cease;
For Summer has o'erbrimm'd their clammy cells.

Who hath not seen Thee oft amid thy store?
Sometimes whoever seeks abroad may find
Thee sitting careless on a granary floor,
Thy hair soft-lifted by the winnowing wind;
Or on a half-reap'd furrow sound asleep,
Drowsed with the fume of poppies, while thy hook
Spares the next swath and all its twinèd flowers;
And sometime like a gleaner thou dost keep
Steady thy laden head across a brook;
Or by a cider-press, with patient look,
Thou watchest the last oozings, hours by hours.

Where are the songs of Spring? Ay, where are they!
Think not of them,—thou hast thy music too,
While barréd clouds bloom the soft-dying day
And touch the stubble-plains with rosy hue;
Then in a wailful choir the small gnats mourn
Among the river-sallows, borne aloft
Or sinking as the light wind lives or dies;
And full-grown lambs loud bleat from hilly bourn;
Hedge-crickets sing; and now with treble soft
The redbreast whistles from a garden-croft,
And gathering swallows twitter in the skies.

J. Keats.

AUTUMN WOODS.

Ere, in the northern gale,
The summer tresses of the trees are gone,
The woods of autumn, all around our vale,
    Have put their glory on.

    The mountains that infold
In their wide sweep the coloured landscape round,
Seem groups of giant kings in purple and gold,
    That guard the enchanted ground.

    I roam the woods that crown
The upland, where the mingled splendours glow,
Where the gay company of trees look down
    On the green fields below.

    My steps are not alone
In these bright walks; the sweet southwest at play
Flies, rustling, where the painted leaves are strown
    Along the winding way.

    And far in heaven, the while,
The sun, that sends that gale to wander here,
Pours out on the fair earth his quiet smile,—
    The sweetest of the year.

    Where now the solemn shade,
Verdure and gloom where many branches meet;
So grateful, when the noon of summer made
    The valleys sick with heat?

Let in through all the trees
Come the strange rays; the forest depths are bright;
Their sunny-coloured foliage in the breeze
    Twinkles, like beams of light.

The rivulet, late unseen,
Where bickering through the shrubs its waters run,
Shines with the image of its golden screen,
    And glimmerings of the sun.

But 'neath yon crimson tree,
Lover to listening maid might breathe his flame,
Nor mark, within its roseate canopy,
    Her blush of maiden shame.

Oh, Autumn! why so soon
Depart the hues that make thy forests glad;
Thy gentle wind and thy fair sunny noon,
    And leave thee wild and sad!

Ah, 'twere a lot too blest
For ever in thy coloured shades to stray,
Amidst the kisses of the soft south-west
    To rove and dream for aye;

And leave the vain low strife,
That makes men mad—the tug for wealth and power,
The passions and the cares that wither life,
    And waste its little hour.

William Cullen Bryant.

ODE TO AUTUMN.

I SAW old Autumn in the misty morn
 Stand shadowless like Silence, listening
To silence, for no lonely bird would sing
Into his hollow ear from woods forlorn,
Nor lowly hedge, nor solitary thorn;
Shaking his languid locks all dewy bright
With tangled gossamer that fell by night,
        Pearling his coronet of golden corn.

Where are the songs of Summer?—With the sun,
Oping the dusky eyelids of the south,
Till shade and silence waken up as one,
And Morning sings with a warm odorous mouth.
Where are the merry birds?—Away, away,
On panting wings through the inclement skies,
        Lest owls should prey
        Undazzled at noon-day,
And tear with horny beak their lustrous eyes.

Where are the blooms of Summer?—In the west,
Blushing their last to the last sunny hours,
When the mild Eve by sudden Night is prest
Like tearful Proserpine, snatch'd from her flow'rs
        To a most gloomy breast.
Where is the pride of Summer,—the green prime,—
The many, many leaves all twinkling?—Three
On the moss'd elm; three on the naked lime
Trembling,—and one upon the old oak tree!
   Where is the Dryad's immortality?—
Gone into mournful cypress and dark yew,
Or wearing the long gloomy Winter through
   In the smooth holly's green eternity.

The squirrel gloats o'er his accomplish'd hoard,
The ants have brimm'd their garners with ripe grain,
   And honey bees have stored
The sweets of summer in their luscious cells;
The swallows all have wing'd across the main;
But here the Autumn melancholy dwells,
   And sighs her tearful spells
Amongst the sunless shadows of the plain.
    Alone, alone,
    Upon a mossy stone,
She sits and reckons up the dead and gone,
With the last leaves for a love-rosary;
Whilst all the wither'd world looks drearily,
Like a dim picture of the drownèd past
In the hush'd mind's mysterious far-away,
Doubtful what ghostly thing will steal the last
Into that distance, grey upon the grey.

O go and sit with her, and be o'ershaded
Under the languid downfall of her hair;
She wears a coronal of flowers faded
Upon her forehead, and a face of care;—
There is enough of wither'd everywhere
To make her bower,—and enough of gloom;
There is enough of sadness to invite,
If only for the rose that died, whose doom
Is Beauty's,—she that with the living bloom
Of conscious cheeks most beautifies the light;
There is enough of sorrowing, and quite
Enough of bitter fruits the earth doth bear,—
Enough of chilly droppings from her bowl;
Enough of fear and shadowy despair,
   To frame her cloudy prison for the soul!

                      T. Hood.

COME DOWN, O MAID!

COME down, O maid, from yonder mountain height:
What pleasure lives in height (the shepherd sang)
In height and cold, the splendour of the hills?
But cease to move so near the Heavens, and cease
To glide a sunbeam by the blasted Pine,
To sit a star upon the sparkling spire;
And come, for Love is of the valley, come
For Love is of the valley, come thou down
And find him; by the happy threshold, he,
Or hand in hand with Plenty in the maize,
Or red with spirted purple of the vats,
Or foxlike in the vine; nor cares to walk
With Death and Morning on the silver horns;
Nor wilt thou snare him in the white ravine,
Nor find him dropt upon the firths of ice,
That huddling slant in furrow-cloven falls
To roll the torrent out of dusky doors:
But follow; let the torrent dance thee down
To find him in the valley; let the wild
Lean-headed Eagles yelp alone, and leave
The monstrous ledges there to slope, and spill
Their thousand wreaths of dangling water-smoke,
That like a broken purpose waste in air:
So waste not thou; but come; for all the vales
Await thee; azure pillars of the hearth
Arise to thee; the children call, and I
Thy shepherd pipe, and sweet is every sound,
Sweeter thy voice, but every sound is sweet;
Myriads of rivulets hurrying through the lawn,
The moan of doves in immemorial elms,
And murmuring of innumerable bees.

A. Tennyson.

CHORAL HYMN TO ARTEMIS.

WHEN the hounds of spring are on winter's traces,
  The mother of months in meadow or plain
Fills the shadows and windy places
  With lisp of leaves and ripple of rain;
And the brown bright nightingale amorous
Is half assuaged for Itylus,
For the Thracian ships and the foreign faces,
  The tongueless vigil, and all the pain.

Come with bows bent and with emptying of quivers,
  Maiden most perfect, lady of light,
With a noise of winds and many rivers,
  With a clamour of waters, and with might;
Bind on thy sandals, O thou most fleet,
Over the splendour and speed of thy feet;
For the faint east quickens, the wan west shivers,
  Round the feet of the day and the feet of the night.

Where shall we find her, how shall we sing to her,
  Fold our hands round her knees, and cling?
O that man's heart were as fire and could spring to her,
  Fire, or the strength of the streams that spring!
For the stars and the winds are unto her
As raiment, as songs of the harp-player;
For the risen stars and the fallen cling to her,
  And the south-west wind and the west wind sing.

For winter's rains and ruins are over,
  And all the season of snows and sins;
The days dividing lover and lover,
  The light that loses, the night that wins;
And time remembered is grief forgotten,
And frosts are slain, and flowers begotten,
And in green underwood and cover
  Blossom by blossom the spring begins.

The full streams feed on flower of rushes,
  Ripe grasses trammel a travelling foot,
The faint fresh flame of the young year flushes
  From leaf to flower, and flower to fruit;
And fruit and leaf are as gold and fire
And the oat is heard above the lyre,
And the hoofëd heel of a satyr crushes
  The chesnut husk at the chesnut root.

And Pan by noon and Bacchus by night,
  Fleeter of foot than the fleet-foot kid,
Follows with dancing and fills with delight
  The Mænad and the Bassarid;
And soft as lips that laugh and hide
The laughing leaves of the trees divide,
And screen from seeing and leave in sight
  The god pursuing, the maiden hid.

The ivy falls with the Bacchanal's hair
  Over her eyebrows hiding her eyes;
The wild vine slipping down leaves bare
  Her bright breast shortening into sighs;
The wild vine slips with the weight of its leaves,
But the berried ivy catches and cleaves
To the limbs that glitter, the feet that scare,
  The wolf that follows, the fawn that flies.

Algernon Charles Swinburne.

HYMN OF PAN.

FROM the forests and highlands
  We come, we come;
From the river-girt islands,
  Where loud waves are dumb
Listening to my sweet pipings.
  The wind in the reeds and the rushes,
    The bees on the bells of thyme,
  The birds on the myrtle bushes,
    The cicale above in the lime,
  And the lizards below in the grass,
Were as silent as ever old Tmolus was,
  Listening to my sweet pipings.

Liquid Peneus was flowing,
  And all dark Tempe lay
In Pelion's shadow, outgrowing
  The light of the dying day,
Speeded by my sweet pipings.
  The Sileni and Sylvans and Fauns,
    And the Nymphs of the woods and waves,
  To the edge of the moist river-lawns,
    And the brink of the dewy caves,
And all that did them attend and follow,
Were silent with love,—as you now, Apollo,
  With envy of my sweet pipings.

I sang of the dancing stars,
  I sang of the dædal earth,
And of heaven, and the Giant wars,
  And love, and death, and birth.

And then I changed my pipings,—
Singing how down the vale of Mænalus
  I pursued a maiden, and clasped a reed:
Gods and men, we are all deluded thus;
  It breaks in our bosom, and then we bleed.
All wept—as I think both ye now would,
If envy or age had not frozen your blood—
  At the sorrow of my sweet pipings.

P. B. Shelley.

A MUSICAL INSTRUMENT.

1.

WHAT was he doing, the great god Pan,
  Down in the reeds by the river?
Spreading ruin and scattering ban,
Splashing and paddling with hoofs of a goat,
And breaking the golden lilies afloat
  With the dragon-fly on the river.

2.

He tore out a reed, the great god Pan,
  From the deep cool bed of the river:
The limpid water turbidly ran,
And the broken lilies a-dying lay,
And the dragon-fly had fled away,
  Ere he brought it out of the river.

3.

High on the shore sat the great god Pan,
  While turbidly flowed the river;
And hacked and hewed as a great god can,
With his hard bleak steel at the patient reed,
Till there was not a sign of the leaf indeed
  To prove it fresh from the river.

4.

He cut it short, did the great god Pan,
   (How tall it stood in the river!)
Then drew out the pith, like the heart of a man,
Steadily from the outside ring,
And notched the poor, dry, empty thing
   In holes, as he sat by the river.

5.

"This is the way," laughed the great god Pan,
   (Laughed while he sat by the river,)
"The only way, since gods began
   To make sweet music, they could succeed."
Then, dropping his mouth to a hole in the reed,
   He blew in power by the river.

6.

Sweet, sweet, sweet, O Pan!
   Piercing sweet by the river!
Blinding sweet, O great god Pan!
The sun on the hill forgot to die,
And the lilies revived, and the dragon-fly
   Came back to dream on the river.

7.

Yet half a beast is the great god Pan,
   To laugh as he sits by the river,
Making a poet out of a man:
The true gods sigh for the cost and pain,—
For the reed which grows nevermore again
   As a reed with the reeds in the river.

Elizabeth Barrett Browning.

PERSEPHONE.

SHE stepped upon Sicilian grass,
  Demeter's daughter fresh and fair,
A child of light, a radiant lass,
  And gamesome as the morning air.
The daffodils were fair to see,
They nodded lightly on the lea,
Persephone—Persephone!

Lo! one she marked of rarer growth
  Than orchis or anemone;
For it the maiden left them both,
  And parted from her company.
Drawn nigh, she deemed it fairer still,
And stooped to gather by the rill
The daffodil, the daffodil.

What ailed the meadow that it shook?
  What ailed the air of Sicily?
She wondered by the brattling brook,
  And trembled with the trembling lea.
The coal-black horses rise—they rise:
O mother, mother!" low she cries—
Persephone—Persephone!

"O light, light, light!" she cries, "farewell;
  The coal-black horses wait for me.
O shade of shades, where I must dwell,
  Demeter, mother, far from thee!

Ah, fated doom that I fulfil!
Ah, fateful flower beside the rill!
The daffodil, the daffodil!"

What ails her that she comes not home!
   Demeter seeks her far and wide,
And gloomy-browed doth ceaseless roam
   From many a morn till eventide.
"My life, immortal though it be,
Is nought," she cries, "for want of thee,
Persephone—Persephone!

"Meadows of Enna, let the rain
   No longer drop to feed your rills,
Nor dew refresh the fields again,
   With all their nodding daffodils!
Fade, fade and droop, O lilied lea,
Where thou, dear heart, wert reft from me—
Persephone—Persephone!"

She reigns upon her dusky throne,
   'Mid shades of heroes dread to see;
Among the dead she breathes alone,
   Persephone—Persephone!
Or seated on the Elysian hill
She dreams of earthly daylight still,
And murmurs of the daffodil.

A voice in Hades soundeth clear,
   The shadows mourn and flit below;
It cries—"Thou Lord of Hades, hear,
   And let Demeter's daughter go.
The tender corn upon the lea
Droops in her goddess gloom, when she
Cries for her lost Persephone.

"From land to land she raging flies,
   The green fruit falleth in her wake,
And harvest fields beneath her eyes
   To earth the grain unripened shake.
Arise, and set the maiden free;
Why should the world such sorrow dree
By reason of Persephone?"

He takes the cleft pomegranate seeds:
   "Love, eat with me this parting day;"
Then bids them fetch the coal-black steeds—
   "Demeter's daughter, wouldst away?"
The gates of Hades set her free;
"She will return full soon," saith he—
"My wife, my wife Persephone."

Low laughs the dark king on his throne—
   "I gave her of pomegranate seeds."
Demeter's daughter stands alone
   Upon the fair Eleusian meads.
Her mother meets her. "Hail!" saith she;
"And doth our daylight dazzle thee,
   My love, my child Persephone?

"What moved thee, daughter, to forsake
   Thy fellow-maids that fatal morn,
And give thy dark lord power to take
   Thee living to his realm forlorn?"
Her lips reply without her will,
As one addressed who slumbereth still—
"The daffodil, the daffodil!"

Her eyelids droop with light oppressed,
   And sunny wafts that round her stir,
Her cheek upon her mother's breast—
   Demeter's kisses comfort her.

7*

Calm Queen of Hades, art thou she
Who stepped so lightly on the lea—
Persephone, Persephone?

When, in her destined course, the moon
  Meets the deep shadow of this world,
And labouring on doth seem to swoon
  Through awful wastes of dimness whirled—
Emerged at length, no trace hath she
Of that dark hour of destiny,
Still silvery sweet—Persephone.

The greater world may near the less,
  And draw it through her weltering shade,
But not one biding trace impress
  Of all the darkness that she made;
The greater soul that draweth thee
Hath left his shadow plain to see
On thy fair face, Persephone!

Demeter sighs, but sure 't is well
  The wife should love her destiny:
They part, and yet, as legends tell,
  She mourns her lost Persephone:
While chant the maids of Enna still—
"O fateful flower beside the rill—
  The daffodil, the daffodil!"

Jean Ingelow.

THE OLD FAMILIAR FACES.

I HAVE had playmates, I have had companions
In my days of childhood, in my joyful school-days;
All, all are gone, the old familiar faces.

I have been laughing, I have been carousing,
Drinking late, sitting late, with my bosom cronies;
All, all are gone, the old familiar faces.

I loved a Love once, fairest among women:
Closed are her doors on me, I must not see her—
All, all are gone, the old familiar faces.

I have a friend, a kinder friend has no man:
Like an ingrate, I left my friend abruptly;
Left him, to muse on the old familiar faces.

Ghost-like I paced round the haunts of my childhood,
Earth seem'd a desert I was bound to traverse,
Seeking to find the old familiar faces.

Friend of my bosom, thou more than a brother,
Why wert not thou born in my father's dwelling?
So might we talk of the old familiar faces,

How some they have died, and some they have left me,
And some are taken from me; all are departed;
All, all are gone, the old familiar faces.

Charles Lamb.

THE LETTERS OF MY YOUTH.

LOOK at the leaves I gather up in trembling—
Little to see, and sere, and time-bewasted,
But they are other than the tree can bear now,
    For they are mine!

Deep as the tumult in an archèd sea-cave,
Out of the Past these antiquated voices
Fall on my heart's ear; I must listen to them,
    For they are mine!

Whose is this hand that wheresoe'er it wanders,
Traces in light words thoughts that come as lightly!
Who was the king of all this soul-dominion?
    I? Was it mine?

With what a healthful appetite of spirit
Sits he at Life's inevitable banquet,
Tasting delight in everything before him!
    Could this be mine?

See how he twists his coronals of fancy
Out of all blossoms, knowing not the poison—
How his young eye is meshed in the enchantment!
    And it was mine!

What, is this I?—this miserable complex
Losing and gaining, only knit together
By the ever-bursting fibres of remembrance—
  What is this *mine?*

Surely we *are* by feeling as by knowing—
Changing our hearts our being changes with them;
Take them away—these spectres of my boyhood;
  They are not mine.

      Lord Houghton.

ONE YEAR AGO.

  ONE year ago my path was green,
My footstep light, my brow serene;
Alas! and could it have been so
  One year ago?

There is a love that is to last
When the hot days of youth are past:
Such love did a sweet maid bestow
  One year ago.

I took a leaflet from her braid
And gave it to another maid.
Love! broken should have been thy bow
  One year ago.

      Walter Savage Landor.

THE DAYS THAT ARE NO MORE.

"TEARS, idle tears, I know not what they mean,
  Tears from the depth of some divine despair
  Rise in the heart, and gather to the eyes,
  In looking on the happy Autumn-fields,
  And thinking of the days that are no more.

"Fresh as the first beam glittering on a sail
  That brings our friends up from the underworld,
  Sad as the last which reddens over one
  That sinks with all we love below the verge;
  So sad, so fresh, the days that are no more.

"Ah, sad and strange as in dark summer dawns
  The earliest pipe of half-awaken'd birds
  To dying ears, when unto dying eyes
  The casement slowly grows a glimmering square;
  So sad, so strange, the days that are no more.

"Dear as remember'd kisses after death,
  And sweet as those by hopeless fancy feign'd
  On lips that are for others; deep as love,
  Deep as first love, and wild with all regret;
  O Death in Life, the days that are no more!"

A. Tennyson.

SONG.

A WIDOW bird sate mourning for her Love
  Upon a wintry bough;
The frozen wind crept on above,
  The freezing stream below.

There was no leaf upon the forest bare,
  No flower upon the ground,
And little motion in the air
  Except the mill-wheel's sound.

P. B. Shelley.

DESERTED.

YE banks and braes o' bonnie Doon,
  How can ye bloom sae fair!
How can ye chant, ye little birds,
  And I sae fu' o' care!

Thou'll break my heart, thou bonnie bird
  That sings upon the bough;
Thou minds me o' the happy days
  When my fause Luve was true.

Thou'll break my heart, thou bonnie bird
  That sings beside thy mate;
For sae I sat, and sae I sang,
  And wist na o' my fate.

Aft hae I roved by bonnie **Doon**
  To see the woodbine twine,
And ilka bird sang o' its love;
  And sae did I o' mine.

Wi' lightsome heart I pu'd **a rose,**
  Frae aff its thorny tree;
And my fause luver staw **the rose,**
  But left the thorn wi' me.
                   R. Burns.

THE HOLLOW OAK.

HOLLOW is the oak beside the sunny **waters drooping;**
Thither came, when I was young, happy **children trooping;**
Dream I now, or hear I now—far, their **mellow whooping!**

Gay below the cowslip bank, see the billow **dances;**
There I lay, beguiling time—when I liv'd **romances;**
Dropping pebbles in the wave, fancies into **fancies;—**

Farther, where the river glides by the wooded **cover,**
Where the merlin singeth low, with the hawk **above her,**
Came a foot and shone a smile—woe is me, **the Lover!**

Leaflets on the hollow oak still as greenly quiver;
Musical amid the reeds murmurs on the river;
But the footstep and the smile?—woe is me for ever!
                Edward Bulwer, Lord Lytton.

DIRGE.

IF thou wilt ease thine heart
Of love and all its smart,
    Then sleep, dear, sleep;
And not a sorrow
  Hang any tear on your eyelashes;
    Lie still and deep,
    Sad soul, until the sea-wave washes
The rim o' the sun to-morrow
    In eastern sky.

But wilt thou cure thine heart
Of love and all its smart,
    Then die, dear, die;
'Tis deeper, sweeter,
  Than on a rose-bank to lie dreaming
    With folded eye;
  And alone amid the beaming
Of love's stars, thou'lt meet her
    In eastern sky.

Thomas Lovell Beddoes.

A LAMENT.

SWIFTER far than summer's flight,
Swifter far than youth's delight,
Swifter far than happy night,
    Art thou come and gone:
As the earth when leaves are dead,
As the night when sleep is sped,
As the heart when joy is fled,
    I am left lone, alone.

The swallow Summer comes again,
The owlet Night resumes her reign,
But the wild swan Youth is fain
    To fly with thee, false as thou:
My heart each day desires the morrow:
Sleep itself is turned to sorrow;
Vainly would my winter borrow
    Sunny leaves from any bough.

Lilies for a bridal bed,
Roses for a matron's head,
Violets for a maiden dead,
    Pansies let my flowers be:
On the living grave I bear
Scatter them without a tear,
Let no friend, however dear,
    Waste one hope, one fear, for me.

P. B. Shelley.

THE BRIDGE OF SIGHS.

ONE more Unfortunate
Weary of breath,
Rashly importunate,
Gone to her death!

Take her up tenderly,
Lift her with care;
Fashion'd so slenderly,
Young, and so fair!

Look at her garments
Clinging like cerements;
Whilst the wave constantly
Drips from her clothing;
Take her up instantly,
Loving, not loathing.—

Touch her not scornfully;
Think of her mournfully,
Gently and humanly;
Not of the stains of her,
All that remains of her
Now is pure womanly.

Make no deep scrutiny
Into her mutiny
Rash and undutiful:
Past all dishonour,
Death has left on her
Only the beautiful.

Still, for all slips of hers,
One of Eve's family—
Wipe those poor lips of hers
Oozing so clammily.

Loop up her tresses
Escaped from the comb,
Her fair auburn tresses;
Whilst wonderment guesses
Where was her home?

Who was her father?
Who was her mother?
Had she a sister?
Had she a brother?
Or was there a dearer one
Still, and a nearer one
Yet, than all other?

Alas! for the rarity
Of Christian charity
Under the sun!
O! it was pitiful!
Near a whole city full,
Home she had none.

Sisterly, brotherly,
Fatherly, motherly
Feelings had changed:
Love, by harsh evidence,
Thrown from its eminence;
Even God's providence
Seeming estranged.

Where the lamps quiver
So far in the river,

With many a light
From window and casement,
From garret to basement,
She stood, with amazement,
Houseless by night.

The bleak wind of March
Made her tremble and shiver;
But not the dark arch,
Or the black flowing river:
Mad from life's history,
Glad to death's mystery,
Swift to be hurl'd—
Any where, any where
Out of the world!

In she plunged boldly,
No matter how coldly
The rough river ran,—
Over the brink of it,
Picture it—think of it,
Dissolute Man!
Lave in it, drink of it,
Then, if you can!

Take her up tenderly,
Lift her with care;
Fashion'd so slenderly,
Young, and so fair!

Ere her limbs frigidly
Stiffen too rigidly,
Decently,—kindly,—
Smoothe, and compose them,
And her eyes, close them,
Staring so blindly!

Dreadfully staring
Thro' muddy impurity,
As when with the daring
Last look of despairing
Fix'd on futurity.

Perishing gloomily,
Spurr'd by contumely,
Cold inhumanity,
Burning insanity,
Into her rest.
—Cross her hands humbly
As if praying dumbly,
Over her breast!

Owning her weakness,
Her evil behaviour,
And leaving, with meekness,
Her sins to her Saviour!

T. Hood.

THE DESERTED HOUSE.

LIFE and Thought have gone away
　　Side by side,
　　Leaving door and windows wide:
Careless tenants they!

All within is dark as night:
In the windows is no light;
And no murmur at the door,
So frequent on its hinge before.

Close the door, the shutters close,
　　Or through the windows we shall see
　　The nakedness and vacancy
Of the dark deserted house.

Come away: no more of mirth
　　Is here, or merry-making sound.
The house was builded of the earth,
　　And shall fall again to ground.

Come away: for life and thought
　　Here no longer dwell:
　　But in a city glorious—
A great and distant city—have bought
　　A mansion incorruptible.
　　　　Would they could have stayed with us!

A. Tennyson.

AFTER DEATH.

THANK Heaven! the crisis,
    The danger is past,
And the lingering illness
    Is over at last—
And the fever called "Living"
    Is conquered at last.

Sadly, I know,
    I am shorn of my strength,
And no muscle I move,
    As I lie at full length—
But no matter!—I feel
    I am better at length.

And I rest so composedly,
    Now, in my bed,
That any beholder
    Might fancy me dead—
Might start at beholding me,
    Thinking me dead.

The moaning and groaning,
    The sighing and sobbing,

Are quieted now,
    With that horrible throbbing
At heart;—ah, that horrible,
    Horrible throbbing!

The sickness—the nausea—
    The pitiless pain—
Have ceased, with the fever
    That maddened my brain—
With the fever called "Living"
    That burned in my brain.

And oh! of all tortures,
    That torture the worst,
Has abated—the terrible
    Torture of thirst,
For the napthaline river
    Of Passion accurst!
I have drunk of a water
    That quenches all thirst:

Of a water that flows
    With a lullaby sound
From a spring but a very few
    Feet under ground—
From a cavern not very far
    Down under ground.

And ah! let it never
    Be foolishly said
That my room it is gloomy,
    And narrow my bed;
For man never slept

In a different bed—
And, to *sleep*, you must slumber
    In just such a bed.

My tantalized spirit
    Here blandly reposes,
Forgetting, or never
    Regretting, its roses—
Its old agitations
    Of myrtles and roses.

For now, while so quietly
    Lying, it fancies
A holier odour
    About it, of pansies—
A rosemary odour,
    Commingled with pansies—
With rue and the beautiful
    Puritan pansies.

And so it lies happily,
    Bathing in many
A dream of the truth
    And the beauty of Annie—
Drowned in a bath
    Of the tresses of Annie.

She tenderly kissed me,
    She fondly caressed,
And then I fell gently
    To sleep on her breast—
Deeply to sleep
    On the heaven of her breast.

When the light was extinguished,
　　She covered me warm,
And she prayed to the angels
　　To keep me from harm—
To the queen of the angels
　　To shield me from harm.

And I lie so composedly,
　　Now, in my bed,
(Knowing her love)
　　That you fancy me dead;
And I rest so contentedly,
　　Now, in my bed,
(With her love at my breast)
　　That you fancy me dead—
That you shudder to look at me,
　　Thinking me dead.

But my heart it is brighter
　　Than all of the many
Stars in the sky,
　　For it sparkles with Annie—
It glows with the light
　　Of the love of my Annie—
With the thought of the light
　　Of the eyes of my Annie.

Edgar Allan Poe.

INTIMATIONS OF IMMORTALITY
FROM RECOLLECTIONS OF EARLY CHILDHOOD.

THERE was a time when meadow, grove, and stream,
The earth, and every common sight
    To me did seem
  Apparelled in celestial light,
The glory and the freshness of a dream.
It is not now as it has been of yore;—
    Turn wheresoe'er I may,
      By night or day,
The things which I have seen I now can see no more!

    The rainbow comes and goes,
    And lovely is the rose;
    The moon doth with delight
Look round her when the heavens are bare;
    Waters on a starry night
    Are beautiful and fair;
  The sunshine is a glorious birth;
  But yet I know, where'er I go,
That there hath pass'd away a glory from the earth.

Now, while the birds thus sing a joyous song,
    And while the young lambs bound
    As to the tabor's sound,
To me alone there came a thought of grief:
A timely utterance gave that thought relief,
    And I again am strong.

The cataracts blow their trumpets from the steep,—
No more shall grief of mine the season wrong:
I hear the echoes through the mountains throng,
The winds come to me from the fields of sleep,
  And all the earth is gay;
   Land and sea
 Give themselves up to jollity,
  And with the heart of May
Doth every beast keep holiday;—
   Thou child of joy
Shout round me, let me hear thy shouts, thou happy
 Shepherd boy!

Ye blessèd creatures, I have heard the call
 Ye to each other make; I see
The heavens laugh with you in your jubilee;
 My heart is at your festival,
 My head hath its coronal,
The fulness of your bliss, I feel—I feel it all.
  O evil day! if I were sullen
  While Earth herself is adorning
   This sweet May morning;
  And the children are pulling
   On every side
  In a thousand valleys far and wide
  Fresh flowers; while the sun shines warm,
And the babe leaps up on his mother's arm:—
  I hear, I hear, with joy I hear!
  —But there's a tree, of many, one,
A single field which I have look'd upon,
Both of them speak of something that is gone:
   The pansy at my feet
   Doth the same tale repeat:
Whither is fled the visionary gleam?
Where is it now, the glory and the dream?

Our birth is but a sleep and a forgetting;
The Soul that rises with us, our life's Star,
    Hath had elsewhere its setting
      And cometh from afar;
    Not in entire forgetfulness,
    And not in utter nakedness,
But trailing clouds of glory do we come
      From God, who is our home:
Heaven lies about us in our infancy!
Shades of the prison-house begin to close
      Upon the growing boy,
But he beholds the light, and whence it flows,
      He sees it in his joy;
The youth, who daily farther from the east
    Must travel, still is Nature's priest,
      And by the vision splendid
      Is on his way attended;
At length the man perceives it die away,
And fade into the light of common day.

Earth fills her lap with pleasures of her own;
Yearnings she hath in her own natural kind,
And, even with something of a mother's mind
      And no unworthy aim,
    The homely nurse doth all she can
To make her foster-child, her inmate, Man,
      Forget the glories he hath known
And that imperial palace whence he came.

Behold the Child among his newborn blisses,
A six years' darling of a pigmy size!
See, where 'mid work of his own hand he lies,
Fretted by sallies of his mother's kisses,
With light upon him from his father's eyes!
See, at his feet, some little plan or chart,
Some fragment from his dream of human life,
Shaped by himself with newly-learnèd art;

A wedding or a festival,
A mourning or a funeral;
      And this hath now his heart,
      And unto this he frames his song:
      Then will he fit his tongue
To dialogues of business, love, or strife;
      But it will not be long
      Ere this be thrown aside,
      And with new joy and pride
The little actor cons another part;
Filling from time to time his 'humorous stage'
With all the Persons, down to palsied Age,
That life brings with her in her equipage;
      As if his whole vocation
      Were endless imitation.

Thou, whose exterior semblance doth belie
      Thy soul's immensity;
Thou best philosopher, who yet dost keep   '
Thy heritage, thou eye among the blind,
That, deaf and silent, read'st the eternal deep,
Haunted for ever by the eternal Mind,—
      Mighty Prophet! Seer blest!
      On whom those truths do rest
Which we are toiling all our lives to find;
Thou, over whom thy immortality
Broods like the day, a master o'er a slave,
A presence which is not to be put by;
Thou little child, yet glorious in the might
Of heaven-born freedom on thy being's height,
Why with such earnest pains dost thou provoke
The years to bring the inevitable yoke,
Thus blindly with thy blessedness at strife?
Full soon thy soul shall have her earthly freight,
And custom lie upon thee with a weight
Heavy as frost, and deep almost as life!

O joy! that in our embers
Is something that doth live,
That Nature yet remembers
What was so fugitive!
The thought of our past years in me doth breed
Perpetual benediction: not indeed
For that which is most worthy to be blest,
Delight and liberty, the simple creed
Of childhood, whether busy or at rest,
With new-fledged hope still fluttering in his breast:
    —Not for these I raise
    The song of thanks and praise;
  But for those obstinate questionings
  Of sense and outward things,
  Fallings from us, vanishings,
  Blank misgivings of a creature
Moving about in worlds not realized,
High instincts, before which our mortal nature
Did tremble like a guilty thing surprized:
  But for those first affections,
  Those shadowy recollections,
    Which, be they what they may,
Are yet the fountain-light of all our day,
Are yet a master-light of all our seeing;
  Uphold us—cherish—and have power to make
Our noisy years seem moments in the being
Of the eternal silence: truths that wake
    To perish never;
Which neither listlessness, nor mad endeavour,
    Nor man, nor boy,
Nor all that is at enmity with joy,
Can utterly abolish or destroy!
  Hence, in a season of calm weather
  Though inland far we be,
Our souls have sight of that immortal sea
  Which brought us hither;
  Can in a moment travel thither—

And see the children sport upon the shore,
And hear the mighty waters rolling evermore.

Then, sing ye birds, sing, sing a joyous song!
     And let the young lambs bound
     As to the tabor's sound!
We, in thought, will join your throng,
     Ye that pipe and ye that play,
     Ye that through your hearts to-day
     Feel the gladness of the May!
What though the radiance which was once so bright
Be now for ever taken from my sight,
     Though nothing can bring back the hour
Of splendour in the grass, of glory in the flower;
     We will grieve not, rather find
     Strength in what remains behind,
     In the primal sympathy
     Which having been must ever be,
     In the soothing thoughts that spring
     Out of human suffering,
     In the faith that looks through death,
In years that bring the philosophic mind.

And O, ye Fountains, Meadows, Hills, and Groves,
Forbode not any severing of our loves!
Yet in my heart of hearts I feel your might;
I only have relinquish'd one delight
To live beneath your more habitual sway;
I love the brooks which down their channels fret
Even more than when I tripp'd lightly as they;
The innocent brightness of a new-born day
     Is lovely yet;
The clouds that gather round the setting sun
Do take a sober colouring from an eye
That hath kept watch o'er man's mortality;
Another race hath been, and other palms are won.

Thanks to the human heart by which **we live,**
Thanks to its tenderness, its joys, **and fears,**
To me the meanest flower that blows **can give**
Thoughts that do often lie too deep **for tears.**

W. Wordsworth.

THE POET'S INVOCATION.

EARTH, Ocean, Air, beloved brotherhood!
If our great Mother has imbued my soul
With aught of natural piety to feel
Your love, and recompense the boon with mine;
If dewy morn, and odorous noon, and even,
With sunset and its gorgeous ministers,
And solemn midnight's tingling silentness;
If Autumn's hollow sighs in the sere wood,
And Winter robing with pure snow and crowns
Of starry ice the grey grass and bare boughs—
If Spring's voluptuous pantings when she breathes
Her first sweet kisses—have been dear to me;
If no bright bird, insect, or gentle beast,
I consciously have injured, but still loved
And cherished these my kindred;—then forgive
This boast, belovèd brethren, and withdraw
No portion of your wonted favour now!

Mother of this unfathomable world,
Favour my solemn song! for I have loved
Thee ever, and thee only; I have watched
Thy shadow, and the darkness of thy steps,
And my heart ever gazes on the depth
Of thy deep mysteries. I have made my bed
In charnels and on coffins, where black Death

Keeps record of the trophies won from thee;
Hoping to still these obstinate questionings
Of thee and thine by forcing some lone ghost,
Thy messenger, to render up the tale
Of what we are. In lone and silent hours,
When night makes a weird sound of its own stillness,
Like an inspired and desperate alchemist
Staking his very life on some dark hope,
Have I mixed awful talk and asking looks
With my most innocent love; until strange tears,
Uniting with those breathless kisses, made
Such magic as compels the charmèd night
To render up thy charge. And, though ne'er yet
Thou hast unveiled thy inmost sanctuary,
Enough from incommunicable dream,
And twilight phantasms, and deep noonday thought,
Has shone within me, that serenely now
And moveless (as a long-forgotten lyre
Suspended in the solitary dome
Of some mysterious and deserted fane)
I wait thy breath, Great Parent; that my strain
May modulate with murmurs of the air,
And motions of the forests and the sea,
And voice of living beings, and woven hymns
Of night and day, and the deep heart of man.

P. B. Shelley.

HYMN TO THE EARTH.

HEXAMETERS.

EARTH! thou mother of numberless children, the nurse and
    the mother,
Hail! O Goddess, thrice hail! Blest be thou! and, blessing,
    I hymn thee!
Forth, ye sweet sounds! from my harp, and my voice shall
    float on your surges—
Soar thou aloft, O my soul! and bear up my song on thy
    pinions.

Travelling the vale with mine eyes—green meadows and
    lake with green island,
Dark in its basin of rock, and the bare stream flowing in
    brightness—
Thrilled with thy beauty and love in the wooded slope of
    the mountain,
Here, great mother, I lie, thy child, with his head on thy
    bosom!
Playful the spirits of noon, that rushing soft through thy
    tresses,
Green-haired goddess! refresh me; and hark! as they hurry
    or linger,
Fill the pause of my harp, or sustain it with musical murmurs,
Into my being thou murmurest joy, and tenderest sadness
Shedd'st thou, like dew, on my heart, till the joy and the
    heavenly sadness
Pour themselves forth from my heart in tears, and the hymn
    of thanksgiving.

Earth! thou mother of numberless children, the nurse and
    the mother,
Sister thou of the stars, and beloved by the sun, the rejoicer!
Guardian and friend of the moon, O Earth, whom the comets
    forget not,
Yea, in the measureless distance wheel round and again they
    behold thee!
Fadeless and young (and what if the latest birth of creation?)
Bride and consort of Heaven, that looks down upon thee
    enamoured!
Say, mysterious Earth! O say, great mother and goddess,
Was it not well with thee then, when first thy lap was un-
    girdled,
Thy lap to the genial Heaven, the day that he wooed thee
    and won thee!
Fair was thy blush, the fairest and first of the blushes of
    morning!
Deep was the shudder, O Earth! the throe of thy self-re-
    tention:
Inly thou strovest to flee, and didst seek thyself at thy centre!
Mightier far was the joy of thy sudden resilience; and forth-
    with
Myriad myriads of lives teemed forth from the mighty em-
    bracement.
Thousand-fold tribes of dwellers, impelled by thousand-fold
    instincts,
Filled, as a dream, the wide waters; the rivers sang on their
    channels;
Laughed on their shores the hoarse seas; the yearning ocean
    swelled upward;
Young life lowed through the meadows, the woods, and the
    echoing mountains,
Wandered bleating in valleys, and warbled on blossoming
    branches.

S. T. Coleridge.

TO THE DAISY.

WITH little here to do or see
Of things that in the great world be,
Sweet Daisy! oft I talk to thee
    For thou art worthy,
Thou unassuming commonplace
Of Nature, with that homely face,
And yet with something of a grace
    Which love makes for thee!

Oft on the dappled turf at ease
I sit and play with similes,
Loose types of things through all degrees,
    Thoughts of thy raising;
And many a fond and idle name
I give to thee, for praise or blame
As is the humour of the game,
    While I am gazing.

A nun demure, of lowly port;
Or sprightly maiden, of Love's court,
In thy simplicity the sport
    Of all temptations;
A queen in crown of rubies drest;
A starveling in a scanty vest;
Are all, as seems to suit thee best,
    Thy appellations.

A little Cyclops, with one eye
Staring to threaten and defy,
That thought comes next—and instantly
  The freak is over,
The shape will vanish, and behold!
A silver shield with boss of gold
That spreads itself, some fairy bold
  In fight to cover.

I see thee glittering from afar—
And then thou art a pretty star,
Not quite so fair as many are
  In heaven above thee!
Yet like a star, with glittering crest,
Self-poised in air thou seem'st to rest;—
May peace come never to his nest
  Who shall reprove thee!

Sweet Flower! for by that name at last
When all my reveries are past
I call thee, and to that cleave fast,
  Sweet silent Creature!
That breath'st with me in sun and air,
Do thou, as thou art wont, repair
My heart with gladness, and a share
  Of thy meek nature!

W. Wordsworth.

A DEAD ROSE.

O ROSE! who dares to name thee?
No longer roseate now, nor soft, nor sweet;
But barren, and hard, and dry as stubble-wheat,
　　Kept seven years in a drawer—thy titles shame thee.

The breeze that used to blow thee
Between the hedge-row thorns, and take away
An odour up the lane, to last all day—
　　If breathing now—unsweetened would forego thee.

The sun that used to smite thee,
And mix his glory in thy gorgeous urn,
Till beam appeared to bloom and flower to burn—
　　If shining now—with not a hue would light thee.

The dew that used to wet thee,
And, white first, grew incarnadined, because
It lay upon thee where the crimson was—
　　If dropping now—would darken where it met thee.

The fly that lit upon thee,
To stretch the tendrils of its tiny feet
Along the leaf's pure edges after heat,—
　　If lighting now—would coldly overrun thee.

The bee that once did suck thee,
And build thy perfumed ambers up his hive,
And swoon in thee for joy, till scarce alive—
    If passing now—would blindly overlook thee.

The heart doth recognise thee,
Alone, alone! The heart doth smell thee sweet,
Doth view thee fair, doth judge thee most complete—
    Though seeing now those changes that disguise thee.

Yes, and the heart doth owe thee
More love, dead rose! than to such roses bold
As Julia wears at dances, smiling cold!—
    Lie still upon this heart, which breaks below thee!

E. B. Browning.

THE DAFFODILS.

I WANDERED lonely as a cloud
That floats on high o'er vales and hills,
When all at once I saw a crowd,
A host, of golden daffodils;
Beside the lake, beneath the trees,
Fluttering and dancing in the breeze.

Continuous as the stars that shine
And twinkle on the milky way,
They stretched in never-ending line
Along the margin of a bay:
Ten thousand saw I at a glance,
Tossing their heads in sprightly dance.

The waves beside them danced; but they
Out-did the sparkling waves in glee:
A poet could not but be gay,
In such a jocund company:
I gazed—and gazed—but little thought
What wealth the show to me had brought:

For oft, when on my couch I lie
In vacant or in pensive mood,
They flash upon that inward eye
Which is the bliss of solitude;
And then my heart with pleasure fills,
And dances with the daffodils.

W. Wordsworth.

SEA MEWS IN WINTER-TIME.

I WALKED beside a dark grey sea,
   And said, "O world, how cold thou art!
Thou poor white world, I pity thee,
   For joy and warmth from thee depart.

"Yon rising wave licks off the snow,
   Winds on the crag each other chase,
In little powdery whirls they blow
   The misty fragments down its face.

"The sea is cold, and dark its rim,
   Winter sits cowering on the wold,
And I beside this watery brim
   Am also lonely, also cold."

I spoke, and drew toward a rock
   Where many mews made twittering sweet;
Their wings upreared, the clustering flock
   Did pat the sea-grass with their feet.

A rock but half submerged, the sea
   Ran up and washed it while they fed;
Their fond and foolish ecstasy
   A wondering in my fancy bred.

Joy companied with every cry,
   Joy in their food, in that keen wind,
That heaving sea, that shaded sky,
   And in themselves, and in their kind.

The phantoms of the deep at play!
  What idlesse graced the twittering things;
Luxurious paddlings in the spray,
  And delicate lifting up of wings.

Then all at once a flight, and fast
  The lovely crowd flew out to sea;
If mine own life had been recast,
  Earth had not looked more changed to me.

"Where is the cold? Yon clouded skies
  Have only dropt their curtains low
To shade the old mother where she lies
  Sleeping a little, neath the snow.

"The cold is not in crag, nor scar,
  Not in the snows that lap the lea,
Not in yon wings that beat afar,
  Delighting, on the crested sea;

"No, nor in yon exultant wind
  That shakes the oak and bends the pine,
Look near, look in, and thou shalt find
  No sense of cold, fond fool, but thine!"

With that I felt the gloom depart,
  And thoughts within me did unfold,
Whose sunshine warmed me to the heart—
  I walked in joy, and was not cold.

                                    J. Ingelow.

TO A SKYLARK.

HAIL to thee, blithe Spirit!
  Bird thou never wert,
That from heaven, or near it,
  Pourest thy full heart
ι profuse strains of unpremeditated art.

Higher still and higher
  From the earth thou springest
Like a cloud of fire;
  The blue deep thou wingest,
nd singing still dost soar, and soaring ever singest.

In the golden lightning
  Of the sunken sun
O'er which clouds are brightening,
  Thou dost float and run,
ke an unbodied joy whose race is just begun.

The pale purple even
  Melts around thy flight;
Like a star of heaven
  In the broad daylight
hou art unseen, but yet I hear thy shrill delight:

Keen as are the arrows
  Of that silver sphere,
Whose intense lamp narrows
  In the white dawn clear
ntil we hardly see, we feel that it is there.

All the earth and air
  With thy voice is loud,
As, when night is bare,
  From one lonely cloud
The moon rains out her beams, and heaven is overflo

What thou art we know not;
  What is most like thee?
From rainbow clouds there flow not
  Drops so bright to see
As from thy presence showers a rain of melody.

Like a poet hidden
  In the light of thought,
Singing hymns unbidden,
  Till the world is wrought
To sympathy with hopes and fears it heeded not:

Like a high-born maiden
  In a palace tower,
Soothing her love-laden
  Soul in secret hour
With music sweet as love, which overflows her bower

Like a glow-worm golden
  In a dell of dew,
Scattering unbeholden
  Its aerial hue
Among the flowers and grass, which screen it from the

Like a rose embower'd
  In its own green leaves,
By warm winds deflower'd,
  Till the scent it gives
Makes faint with too much sweet these heavy-wingèd th

Sound of vernal showers
    On the twinkling grass,
Rain-awaken'd flowers,
    All that ever was
Joyous, and clear, and fresh, thy music doth surpass.

Teach us, sprite or bird,
    What sweet thoughts are thine:
I have never heard
    Praise of love or wine
That panted forth a flood of rapture so divine.

Chorus hymeneal
    Or triumphal chaunt
Match'd with thine, would be all
    But an empty vaunt—
A thing wherein we feel there is some hidden want.

What objects are the fountains
    Of thy happy strain?
What fields, or waves, or mountains?
    What shapes of sky or plain?
What love of thine own kind? what ignorance of pain?

With thy clear keen joyance
    Languor cannot be:
Shadow of annoyance
    Never came near thee:
Thou lovest; but ne'er knew love's sad satiety.

Waking or asleep,
    Thou of death must deem
Things more true and deep
    Than we mortals dream,
Or how could thy notes flow in such a crystal stream?

We look before and after,
  And pine for what is not:
Our sincerest laughter
  With some pain is fraught;
Our sweetest songs are those that tell of saddest thought.

Yet if we could scorn
  Hate, and pride, and fear;
If we were things born
  Not to shed a tear,
I know not how thy joy we ever should come near.

Better than all measures
  Of delightful sound,
Better than all treasures
  That in books are found,
Thy skill to poet were, thou scorner of the ground!

Teach me half the gladness
  That thy brain must know,
Such harmonious madness
  From my lips would flow,
The world should listen then as I am listening now!

                                        P. B. Shelley.

ODE TO A NIGHTINGALE.

1.

My heart aches, and a drowsy numbness pains
   My sense, as though of hemlock I had drunk,
Or emptied some dull opiate to the drains
   One minute past, and Lethe-wards had sunk:
'Tis not through envy of thy happy lot, .
   But being too happy in thy happiness,—
      That thou, light-wingéd Dryad of the trees,
         In some melodious plot
   Of beechen green, and shadows numberless,
      Singest of summer in full-throated ease.

2.

O for a draught of vintage, that hath been
   Cool'd a long age in the deep-delvéd earth,
Tasting of Flora and the country green,
   Dance, and Provençal song, and sun-burnt mirth!
O for a beaker full of the warm South,
   Full of the true, the blushful Hippocrene,
      With beaded bubbles winking at the brim
         And purple-stainéd mouth;
   That I might drink, and leave the world unseen,
      And with thee fade away into the forest dim:

3.

Fade far away, dissolve, and quite forget
   What thou among the leaves hast never known,
The weariness, the fever, and the fret
   Here, where men sit and hear each other groan;

Where palsy shakes a few, sad, last gray hairs,
   Where youth grows pale, and spectre-thin, and dies;
      Where but to think is to be full of sorrow
         And leaden-eyed despairs;
      Where Beauty cannot keep her lustrous eyes,
         Or new Love pine at them beyond to-morrow.

4.

Away! away! for I will fly to thee,
   Not charioted by Bacchus and his pards,
But on the viewless wings of Poesy,
   Though the dull brain perplexes and retards:
Already with thee! tender is the night,
   And haply the Queen-Moon is on her throne,
      Cluster'd around by all her starry Fays;
         But here there is no light
      Save what from heaven is with the breezes blown
         Through verdurous glooms and winding mossy ways.

5.

I cannot see what flowers are at my feet,
   Nor what soft incense hangs upon the boughs,
But, in embalmèd darkness, guess each sweet
   Wherewith the seasonable month endows
The grass, the thicket, and the fruit-tree wild;
   White hawthorn, and the pastoral eglantine;
      Fast-fading violets cover'd up in leaves;
         And mid-May's eldest child,
      The coming musk-rose, full of dewy wine,
         The murmurous haunt of flies on summer eves.

6.

Darkling I listen; and for many a time
   I have been half in love with easeful Death,
Call'd him soft names in many a musèd rhyme,
   To take into the air my quiet breath;

Now more than ever seems it rich to die,
 To cease upon the midnight with no pain,
  While thou art pouring forth thy soul abroad
   In such an ecstasy!
 Still wouldst thou sing, and I have ears in vain—
 To thy high requiem become a sod.

7.

Thou wast not born for death, immortal bird!
 No hungry generations tread thee down;
The voice I hear this passing night was heard
 In ancient days by emperor and clown:
Perhaps the self-same song that found a path
 Through the sad heart of Ruth, when, sick for home,
  She stood in tears amid the alien corn;
   The same that oft-times hath
 Charmed magic casements, opening on the foam
 Of perilous seas, in faëry lands forlorn.

8.

Forlorn! the very word is like a bell
 To toll me back from thee to my sole self!
Adieu! the fancy cannot cheat so well
 As she is famed to do, deceiving elf.
Adieu! adieu! thy plaintive anthem fades
 Past the near meadows, over the still stream,
  Up the hill-side; and now 'tis buried deep
   In the next valley glades:
 Was it a vision, or a waking dream?
 Fled is that music!—Do I wake or sleep?

J. Keats.

TO THE CUCKOO.

O BLITHE new-comer! I have heard,
I hear thee and rejoice:
O Cuckoo! shall I call thee bird,
Or but a wandering voice?

While I am lying on the grass,
Thy loud note smites my ear!
From hill to hill it seems to pass,
At once far off and near!

I hear thee babbling to the vale
Of sunshine and of flowers;
And unto me thou bring'st a tale
Of visionary hours.

Thrice welcome, darling of the spring!
Even yet thou art to me
No bird, but an invisible thing,
A voice, a mystery.

The same whom in my school-boy days
I listened to; that cry
Which made me look a thousand ways
In bush, and tree, and sky.

To seek thee did I often rove
Through woods and on the green;
And thou wert still a hope, a love;
Still longed for, never seen!

And I can listen to thee yet;
Can lie upon the plain
And listen, till I do beget
That golden time again.

O blessed bird! the earth we pace
Again appears to be
An unsubstantial, fairy place,
That is fit home for thee!

W. Wordsworth.

TO A WATERFOWL.

WHITHER, midst falling dew,
While glow the heavens with the last steps of day,
Far through their rosy depths dost thou pursue
    Thy solitary way?

Vainly the fowler's eye
Might mark thy distant flight to do thee wrong,
As, darkly painted on the crimson sky,
    Thy figure floats along.

Seek'st thou the plashy brink
Of weedy lake, or marge of river wide,
Or where the rocking billows rise and sink
    On the chafed ocean side?

There is a Power whose care
Teaches thy way along that pathless coast,—
The desert and illimitable air,—
    Lone wandering, but not lost.

All day thy wings have fanned
At that far height, the cold thin atmosphere;
Yet stoop not, weary, to the welcome land,
    Though the dark night is near.

And soon that toil shall end,
Soon shalt thou find a summer home, and rest,
And scream among thy fellows; reeds shall bend
    Soon o'er thy sheltered nest.

Thou'rt gone, the abyss of heaven
Hath swallowed up thy form; yet on my heart
Deeply hath sunk the lesson thou hast given,
    And shall not soon depart.

He who, from zone to zone,
Guides through the boundless sky thy certain flight,
In the long way that I must tread alone,
    Will lead my steps aright.

                    W. C. Bryant.

THE EAGLE.

HE clasps the crag with crooked hands;
Close to the sun in lonely lands,
Ring'd with the azure world, he stands.

The wrinkled sea beneath him crawls;
He watches from his mountain walls,
And like a thunderbolt he falls.

A. Tennyson.

ITYLUS.

SWALLOW, my sister, O sister swallow,
  How can thine heart be full of the spring?
    A thousand summers are over and dead.
What hast thou found in the spring to follow?
  What hast thou found in thy heart to sing?
    What wilt thou do when the summer is shed?

O swallow, sister, O fair swift swallow,
  Why wilt thou fly after spring to the south,
    The soft south whither thine heart is set?
Shall not the grief of the old time follow?
  Shall not the song thereof cleave to thy mouth?
    Hast thou forgotten ere I forget?

Sister, my sister, O fleet sweet swallow,
  Thy way is long to the sun and the south;
    But I, fulfilled of my heart's desire,
Shedding my song upon height, upon hollow,
  From tawny body and sweet small mouth,
    Feed the heart of the night with fire.

I, the nightingale, all spring through,
  O swallow, sister, O changing swallow,
    All spring through till the spring be done,
Clothed with the light of the night on the dew,
  Sing, while the hours and the wild birds follow,
    Take flight and follow and find the sun.

Sister, my sister, O soft light swallow,
  Though all things feast in the spring's guest-chamber,
    How hast thou heart to be glad thereof yet?
For where thou fliest I shall not follow,
  Till life forget and death remember,
    Till thou remember and I forget.

Swallow, my sister, O singing swallow,
  I know not how thou hast heart to sing.
    Hast thou the heart? Is it all past over?
Thy lord the summer is good to follow,
  And fair the feet of thy lover the spring:
    But what wilt thou say to the spring thy lover?

O swallow, sister, O fleeting swallow,
  My heart in me is a molten ember,
    And over my head the waves have met.
But thou would'st tarry or I would follow,
  Could I forget or thou remember,
    Couldst thou remember and I forget.

O sweet stray sister, O shifting swallow,
　The heart's division divideth us.
　　Thy heart is light as a leaf of a tree;
But mine goes forth among sea-gulfs hollow
　To the place of the slaying of Itylus,
　　The feast of Daulis, the Thracian sea.

O swallow, sister, O rapid swallow,
　I pray thee sing not a little space.
　　Are not the roofs and the lintels wet?
The woven web that was plain to follow,
　The small slain body, the flower-like face,
　　Can I remember if thou forget?

O sister, sister, thy first-begotten!
　The hands that cling and the feet that follow,
　　The voice of the child's blood crying yet
Who hath remembered me? who hath forgotten?
　Thou hast forgotten, O summer swallow,
　　But the world shall end when I forget.

A. C. Swinburne.

SUMMER-TIME.

WHAT is so rare as a day in June?
  Then, if ever, come perfect days;
Then Heaven tries the earth, if it be in tune,
  And over it softly her warm ear lays:
And whether we look, or whether we listen,
We hear life murmur, or see it glisten.
Every clod feels a stir of might,
  An instinct within it that reaches and towers,
And, grasping blindly above it for light,
  Climbs to a soul in grass and flowers;
The flush of life may well be seen
  Thrilling back over woodlands and valleys;
The cowslip startles in meadows green,
  The buttercup catches the sun in its chalice,
And there's never a leaf or a blade too mean
  To be some happy creature's palace.
The little bird sits at his door in the sun,
  Atilt like a blossom among the leaves,
And lets his illumined being o'errun
  With the deluge of summer it receives;
His mate feels the eggs beneath her wings,
And the heart in her dumb breast flutters and sings;
He sings to the wide world, and she to her nest—
In the nice ear of Nature which song is the best?
Now is the high-tide of the year,
  And whatever of life hath ebbed away
Comes flooding back with a ripply cheer
  Into every bare inlet and creek and bay;

Now the heart is so full that a drop o'erfills it,
We are happy now, because God so wills it.
No matter how barren the past may have been,
'Tis enough for us now that the leaves are green;
We sit in the warm shade and feel right well
How the sap creeps up and the blossoms swell;
We may shut our eyes, but we cannot help knowing
That skies are clear and grass is growing;
The breeze comes whispering in our ear
That dandelions are blossoming near,
    That maize has sprouted, that streams are flowing,
That the river is bluer than the sky,
That the robin is plastering his house hard by;
And if the breeze kept the good news back
For other couriers we should not lack;
    We could guess it all by yon heifer's lowing—
And hark! how clear bold chanticleer,
Warmed with the new wine of the year,
    Tells all in his lusty crowing!

James Russell Lowell.

WINTER-TIME.

DOWN swept the chill wind from the mountain-peak,
    From the snow five thousand summers old;
On open wold and hill-top bleak
    It had gathered all the cold,
And whirled it like sleet on the wanderer's cheek;
It carried a shiver everywhere
From the unleafed boughs and pastures bare;
The little brook heard it and built a roof
'Neath which he could house him, winter-proof;
All night by the white stars' frosty gleams
He groined his arches and matched his beams;

Slender and clear were his crystal spars
As the lashes of light that trim the stars;
He sculptured every summer delight
In his halls and chambers out of sight;
Sometimes his tinkling waters slipt
Down through a frost-leaved forest crypt,
Long, sparkling aisles of steel-stemmed trees
Bending to counterfeit a breeze;
Sometimes the roof no fretwork knew
But silvery mosses that downward grew;
Sometimes it was carved in sharp relief
With quaint arabesques of ice-fern leaf;
Sometimes it was simply smooth and clear
For the gladness of Heaven to shine through; **and here**
He had caught the nodding bulrush-tops
And hung them thickly with diamond drops
Which crystalled the beams of moon and sun,
And made a star of every one.
No mortal builder's most rare device
Could match this winter palace of ice;
'Twas as if ev'ry image that mirrored lay
In his depths serene through the summer day,
Each flitting shadow of earth and sky,
   Lest the happy model should be lost,
Had been mimicked in fairy masonry
   By the elfin builders of the frost.

J. R. Lowell.

CHRISTMAS CAROL.

OUTLANDERS, whence come ye last?
  The snow in the street and the wind on the door.
Through what green seas and great have ye past?
  Minstrels and maids, stand forth on the floor.

From far away, O masters mine,
  The snow in the street and the wind on the door.
We come to bear you goodly wine,
  Minstrels and maids, stand forth on the floor.

From far away we come to you,
  The snow in the street and the wind on the door.
To tell of great tidings strange and true,
  Minstrels and maids, stand forth on the floor.

News, news of the Trinity,
  The snow in the street and the wind on the door.
And Mary and Joseph from over the sea!
  Minstrels and maids, stand forth on the floor.

For as we wandered far and wide,
  The snow in the street and the wind on the door.
What hap do ye deem there should us betide!
  Minstrels and maids, stand forth on the floor.

Under a bent when the night was deep,
  The snow in the street and the wind on the door.
There lay three shepherds tending their sheep.
  Minstrels and maids, stand forth on the floor.

"O ye shepherds, what have ye seen,
  The snow in the street and the wind on the door.
To slay your sorrow, and heal your teen?"
  Minstrels and maids, stand forth on the floor.

"In an ox-stall this night we saw,
  The snow in the street and the wind on the door.
A babe and a maid without a flaw.
  Minstrels and maids, stand forth on the floor.

"There was an old man there beside,
  The snow in the street and the wind on the door.
His hair was white and his hood was wide.
  Minstrels and maids, stand forth on the floor.

"And as we gazed this thing upon,
  The snow in the street and the wind on the door.
Those twain knelt down to the Little One.
  Minstrels and maids, stand forth on the floor.

"And a marvellous song we straight did hear,
  The snow in the street and the wind on the door.
That slew our sorrow and healed our care."
  Minstrels and maids, stand forth on the floor.

News of a fair and a marvellous thing,
  The snow in the street and the wind on the door,
Nowell, nowell, nowell, we sing!
  Minstrels and maids, stand forth on the floor.

                              William Morris.

TO THE NEW YEAR.

Dip down upon the northern shore,
 O sweet new-year delaying long;
 Thou doest expectant nature wrong;
Delaying long, delay no more.

What stays thee from the clouded noons,
 Thy sweetness from its proper place?
 Can trouble live with April days,
Or sadness in the summer moons?

Bring orchis, bring the foxglove spire,
 The little speedwell's darling blue,
 Deep tulips dash'd with fiery dew,
Laburnums, dropping-wells of fire.

O thou, new-year, delaying long,
 Delayest the sorrow in my blood,
 That longs to burst a frozen bud
And flood a fresher throat with song.

A. Tennyson.

THE RAINY DAY.

THE day is cold, and dark, and dreary;
It rains, and the wind is never weary;
The vine still clings to the mouldering wall,
But at every gust the dead leaves fall,
   And the day is dark and dreary.

My life is cold, and dark, and dreary;
It rains, and the wind is never weary;
My thoughts still cling to the mouldering Past,
But the hopes of youth fall thick in the blast,
   And the days are dark and dreary.

Be still, sad heart! and cease repining;
Behind the clouds is the sun still shining;
Thy fate is the common fate of all,
Into each life some rain must fall,
   Some days must be dark and dreary.

H. W. Longfellow.

AFTER RAIN.

THE cock is crowing,
The stream is flowing,
The small birds twitter,
The lake doth glitter,
The green field sleeps in the sun;
　The oldest and youngest
　Are at work with the strongest;
The cattle are grazing,
Their heads never raising;
There are forty feeding like one!

Like an army defeated
The Snow hath retreated,
And now doth fare ill
On the top of the bare hill;
The Plough-boy is whooping—anon—anon:
　There's joy in the mountains;
　There's life in the fountains;
Small clouds are sailing,
Blue sky prevailing;
The rain is over and gone!

W. Wordsworth.

MENIE.

AGAIN rejoicing nature sees
  Her robe assume its vernal hues,
Her leafy locks wave in the breeze,
  All freshly steep'd in morning dews.

In vain to me the cowslips blaw,
  In vain to me the violets spring;
In vain to me, in glen or shaw,
  The mavis and the lintwhite sing.

The merry ploughboy cheers his team,
  Wi' joy the tentie seedsman stalks;
But life to me's a weary dream,
  A dream of ane that never wauks.

The wanton coot the water skims,
  Amang the reeds the ducklings cry,
The stately swan majestic swims,
  And every thing is blest but I.

The sheep-herd steeks his faulding slap,
  And owre the moorlands whistles shrill;
Wi' wild, unequal, wand'ring step,
  I meet him on the dewy hill.

And when the lark, 'tween light and dark,
  Blythe waukens by the daisy's side,
And mounts and sings on flittering wings,
  A woe-worn ghaist I hameward glide.

Come, Winter, with thine angry howl,
  And raging bend the naked tree;
Thy gloom will soothe my cheerless soul,
  When nature all is sad like me!

And maun I still on Menie doat,
  And bear the scorn that's in her e'e?
For it's jet, jet black, and it's like a hawk,
  And it winna let a body be!

R. Burns.

THE PRIDE OF YOUTH.

PROUD Maisie is in the wood,
  Walking so early;
Sweet Robin sits on the bush
  Singing so rarely.

"Tell me, thou bonny bird,
  When shall I marry me?"
—"When six braw gentlemen
  Kirkward shall carry ye."

"Who makes the bridal bed,
  Birdie, say truly?"
—"The gray-headed sexton
  That delves the grave duly.

"The glowworm o'er grave and stone
  Shall light thee steady;
The owl from the steeple sing
  Welcome, proud lady."

Sir W. Scott.

O WERE MY LOVE YON LILAC FAIR.

O WERE my love yon lilac fair
  Wi' purple blossoms to the spring;
And I a bird to shelter there,
  When wearied on my little wing:

How I wad mourn, when it was torn
  By autumn wild, and winter rude!
But I wad sing on wanton wing,
  When youthfu' May its bloom renew'd.

O gin my love were yon red rose
  That grows upon the castle wa',
And I mysel' a drap o' dew,
  · Into her bonnie breast to fa'!

Oh! there beyond expression blest,
  I'd feast on beauty a' the night;
Seal'd on her silk-saft faulds to rest,
  Till fley'd awa' by Phœbus' light.

R. Burns.

THE MILLER'S DAUGHTER.

IT is the miller's daughter,
  And she's grown so dear, so dear,
That I would be the jewel
  That trembles at her ear:
For hid in ringlets day and night,
I'd touch her neck so warm and white.

And I would be the girdle
  About her dainty dainty waist,
And her heart would beat against me
  In sorrow and in rest:
And I should know if it beat right,
I'd clasp it round so close and tight.

And I would be the necklace,
  And all day long to fall and rise
Upon her balmy bosom,
  With her laughter or her sighs,
And I would lie so light, so light,
I scarce should be unclasp'd at night.

                  A. Tennyson.

TO HELEN.

HELEN, thy beauty is to me
    Like those Nicéan barks of yore
That gently, o'er a perfumed sea
    The weary, way-worn wanderer bore
    To his own native shore.

On desperate seas long wont to roam,
    Thy hyacinth hair, thy classic face,
Thy Naiad airs have brought me home
    To the glory that was Greece
And the grandeur that was Rome.

Lo, in yon brilliant window-niche
    How statue-like I see thee stand,
    The agate lamp within thy hand!
Ah, Psyche, from the regions which
    Are holy land!

E. A. Poe.

SERENADE.

THERE be none of Beauty's daughters
  With a magic like thee:
And like music on the waters
  Is thy sweet voice to me:
When, as if its sound were causing
The charmèd ocean's pausing,
The waves lie still and gleaming,
And the lull'd winds seem dreaming:

And the midnight moon is weaving
  Her bright chain o'er the deep,
Whose breast is gently heaving
  As an infant's asleep:
So the spirit bows before thee
To listen and adore thee;
With a full but soft emotion,
Like the swell of Summer's ocean.

Lord Byron.

TO ——

MUSIC, when soft voices die,
Vibrates in the memory;
Odours, when sweet violets sicken,
Live within the sense they quicken;

Rose leaves, when the rose is dead,
Are heaped for the belovèd's bed;
And so thy thoughts, when thou art gone,
Love itself shall slumber on.

P. B. Shelley.

MUSIC.

WHEN lovely sounds about my ears
　　Like winds in Eden's tree-tops rise,
And make me, though my spirit hears,
　　For very luxury close my eyes:
Let none but friends be round about,
　　Who love the soothing joy like me,
That so the charm be felt throughout,
　　And all be harmony.

And when we reach the close divine,
　　Then let the hand of her I love
Come with its gentle palm on mine,
　　As soft as snow, or lighting dove;
And let, by stealth, that more than friend
　　Look sweetness in my opening eyes;
For only so such dreams should end,
　　Or wake in Paradise.

L. Hunt.

BUGLE SONG.

THE splendour falls on castle walls
  And snowy summits, old in story:
The long light shakes across the lakes,
  And the wild cataract leaps in glory.
Blow, bugle, blow, set the wild echoes flying,
Blow, bugle; answer, echoes, dying, dying, dying.

O hark, O hear! how thin and clear,
  And thinner, clearer, farther going!
O sweet and far from cliff and scar
  The horns of Elfland faintly blowing!
Blow, let us hear the purple glens replying:
Blow, bugle; answer, echoes, dying, dying, dying.

O love, they die in yon rich sky,
  They faint on hill or field or river:
Our echoes roll from soul to soul,
  And grow for ever and for ever.
Blow, bugle, blow, set the wild echoes flying,
And answer, echoes, answer, dying, dying, dying.

A. Tennyson.

· ECHOES.

How sweet the answer Echo makes
To Music at night
When, roused by lute or horn, she wakes,
And far away o'er lawns and lakes
Goes answering light!

Yet Love hath echoes truer far
And far more sweet
Than e'er, beneath the moonlight's star,
Of horn or lute or soft guitar
The songs repeat.

'Tis when the sigh,—in youth sincere
And only then,
The sigh that's breathed for one to hear—
Is by that one, that only Dear
Breathed back again.

T. Moore.

TWILIGHT.

IT is the hour when from the boughs
 The nightingale's high note is heard;
It is the hour when lovers' vows
 Seem sweet in every whispered word;
And gentle winds, and waters near,
Make music to the lonely ear.
Each flower the dews have lightly wet,
And in the sky the stars are met,
And on the wave is deeper blue,
And on the leaf a browner hue,
And in the heaven that clear obscure,
So softly dark, and darkly pure,
Which follows the decline of day,
As twilight melts beneath the moon away.

Lord Byron.

EVENING.

FROM yonder grove mark blue-eyed Eve proceed:
First through the warm and deep and scented glens,
Through the pale-glimmering privet-scented lane,
And through those alders by the river-side;
Now the soft dust impedes her, which the sheep
Have hollowed out beneath their hawthorn shade.
But ah! look yonder! see a misty tide
Rise up the hill, lay low the frowning grove,
Enwrap the gay white mansion, sap its sides
Until they melt away like chalk;
Now it comes down against our village-tower,
Covers its base, floats o'er its arches, tears
The clinging ivy from the battlements,
Mingles in broad embrace the obdurate stone,
(All one vast ocean,) and goes swelling on
In slow and silent, dim and deepening waves.

Walter Savage Landor.

A NIGHT-PIECE.

     —THE sky is overcast
With a continuous cloud of texture close,
Heavy and wan, all whitened by the Moon
Which through that veil is indistinctly seen,
A dull contracted circle, yielding light
So feebly spread, that not a shadow falls,
Chequering the ground—from rock, plant, tree, or tower.
At length a pleasant instantaneous gleam
Startles the pensive traveller while he treads
His lonesome path, with unobserving eye
Bent earthwards; he looks up—the clouds are split
Asunder,—and above his head he sees
The clear Moon, and the glory of the heavens.
There, in a black-blue vault, she sails along
Followed by multitudes of stars, that, small
And sharp, and bright, along the dark abyss
Drive as she drives: how fast they wheel away,
Yet vanish not!—the wind is in the tree,
But they are silent;—still they roll along
Immeasurably distant; and the vault,
Built round by those white clouds, enormous clouds,
Still deepens its unfathomable depth.
At length the Vision closes; and the mind,
Not undisturbed by the delight it feels,
Which slowly settles into peaceful calm,
Is left to muse upon the solemn scene.

       W. Wordsworth.

NIGHT IN THE DESERT.

How beautiful is night!
A dewy freshness fills the silent air;
No mist obscures, nor cloud, nor speck, nor stain,
Breaks the serene of heaven:
In full orbed glory yonder moon divine
Rolls through the dark blue depths:
Beneath her steady ray
The desert-circle spreads,
Like the round ocean, girdled with the sky.
How beautiful is night!

R. Southey.

TO THE MOON.

ART thou pale for weariness
Of climbing heaven, and gazing on the earth,
Wandering companionless
Among the stars that have a different birth,—
And ever changing, like a joyless eye
That finds no object worth its constancy?

P. B. Shelley.

THE MOON.

How beautiful the Queen of Night, on high
Her way pursuing among scatter'd clouds,
Where, ever and anon, her head she shrouds
Hidden from view in dense obscurity!
But look, and to the watchful eye
A brightening edge will indicate that soon
We shall behold the struggling Moon
Break forth,—again to walk the clear blue sky.

W. Wordsworth.

THE WORLD'S WANDERERS.

TELL me, thou star, whose wings of light
Speed thee in thy fiery flight,
In what cavern of the night
    Will thy pinions close now?

Tell me, moon, thou pale and grey
Pilgrim of heaven's homeless way,
In what depth of night or day
    Seekest thou repose now?

Weary wind, who wanderest
Like the world's rejected guest,
Hast thou still some secret nest
    On the tree or billow?

P. B. Shelley.

HYMN TO THE NIGHT.

Ἀσπασίη, τριλλιστος.

I HEARD the trailing garments of the Night
  Sweep through her marble halls!
I saw her sable skirts all fringed with light
  From the celestial walls!

I felt her presence, by its spell of might,
  Stoop o'er me from above;
The calm, majestic presence of the Night,
  As of the one I love.

I heard the sounds of sorrow and delight,
  The manifold, soft chimes,
That fill the haunted chambers of the Night,
  Like some old poet's rhymes.

From the cool cisterns of the midnight air
  My spirit drank repose;
The fountain of perpetual peace flows there,—
  From those deep cisterns flows.

O holy Night! from thee I learn to bear
  What man has borne before!
Thou layest thy finger on the lips of Care,
  And they complain no more.

Peace! Peace! Orestes-like I breathe this prayer!
  Descend with broad-winged flight,
The welcome, the thrice-prayed for, the most fair,
  The best-belovéd Night!

H. W. Longfellow.

DATUR HORA QUIETI.

THE sun upon the lake is low,
  The wild birds hush their song,
The hills have evening's deepest glow,
  Yet Leonard tarries long.
Now all whom varied toil and care
  From home and love divide,
In the calm sunset may repair
  Each to the loved one's side.

The noble dame on turret high,
  Who waits her gallant knight,
Looks to the western beam to spy
  The flash of armour bright.
The village maid, with hand on brow
  The level ray to shade,
Upon the footpath watches now
  For Colin's darkening plaid.

Now to their mates the wild swans row,
  By day they swam 'apart,
And to the thicket wanders slow
  The hind beside the hart.
The woodlark at his partner's side
  Twitters his closing song—
All meet whom day and care divide,
  But Leonard tarries long!

Sir W. Scott.

MEETING AT NIGHT.

1.

THE grey sea and the long black land;
And the yellow half-moon large and low;
And the startled little waves that leap
In fiery ringlets from their sleep,
As I gain the cove with pushing prow,
And quench its speed in the slushy sand.

2.

Then a mile of warm sea-scented beach;
Three fields to cross till a farm appears;
A tap at a pane, the quick sharp scratch
And blue spurt of a lighted match,
And a voice less loud, thro' its joys and fears,
Than the two hearts beating each to each!

Robert Browning.

PARTING AT MORNING.

ROUND the cape of a sudden came the sea,
And the sun look'd over the mountain's rim:
And straight was a path of gold for him,
And the need of a world of men for me.

R. Browning.

IN THE STORM.

(IN MEMORY OF MY SON. WRITTEN AT
TAYMOUTH, PERTHSHIRE.)

IF, going forth in the snow and the hail,
  In the wind and the rain,
On the desolate hills, in the face of the gale,
  I could meet thee again;

Ah! with what rapture my bosom would beat
  And my steps onward pass,
With a smile on my lip, while the thin driving sleet
  Soaked through the cold grass!

But never—the hour can never have birth
  That would gladden me thus;
There are meetings, and greetings, and welcomes on earth,
  But no more for us!

No more shalt thou comfort the long dreary night,
  Or the brief bitter day;
When my heart feels the pang of a serpent's keen bite
  In the words others say;

No more shall thy letters come in with the morn,
  Making sunshine for hours,
With thoughts of an innocent tenderness born,
  Or a spray of dried flowers!

With praises whose love used to cheer and to bless,
  Running through every line;
And fond closing words that felt like a caress
  Which thy soul gave to mine.

Many missives lie heaped, to be read in their turn.
  Oh! tender and true,
In the blank of that hour how wildly I yearn
  For the writing I knew!

Unmeaning and vapid, or bitter, the words
  Which I blot with vain tears:
Thy pity no longer the solace affords
  Which it gave in past years.

I shall see thee no more, till life's trial shall cease,
  Gliding into my room,
With thy sweet eyes so full of the spirit of peace,
  Soothing anger and gloom.

I shall hear thee no more, with that low gentle voice
  Whose divine music made,
Like the harp of young David, the spirit rejoice
  That was crushed and betrayed.

I fling wide my casement: forth, forth I would roam,
  And I mock at the storm
As it beats, sweeping inward, to visit a home
  All living and warm.

The grey clouds are scudding in vaporous shrouds
  O'er a sky dark as lead:
I think of the tombs that are planted in crowds—
  Pale homes of the dead!

I think, does the same wind that sweeps by me now,
   As it shivers and moans,
Thrill the pools in that graveyard, of half-melted snow,
   By the moss-dripping stones?

And I cry in my anguish, "Appear! as in life,—
   And my soul shall not·fear:—
Pass over this sea of my trouble and strife!"
   But the winds only, hear.

I turn from the casement, and helplessly stare
   At the light of my lamp;
The drift of the sleet on my arms and my hair
   Lieth chilly and damp.

The rush of the wild river rolling along
   Is loud in my ear—
The wind through the beech-trees is heavy and strong,
   But *that* sound cometh clear.

I know that dark river—its waters sweep down,
   Be the day ne'er so bright,
With the deep changeless hues of the Cairngorm's brown,
   Though its foam-flakes are white.

I know that dark river—it swells and it swirls
   Past the hindering bridge;
And the trees topple down as the branches it hurls
   Beat the bank's broken ridge.

The turbulent waters drive on in their force
   Like the thoughts in my breast—
But the stones lying deep in the torrent's wild course
   Say—"Under, is rest!"—

Under—deep under those arches' wide girth,
  Where nothing is stirred,—
And the sound of Life's whirlwinds that traverse the earth
  Can never be heard!

Under—deep under. But lo! while I dream,
  From a vanishing cloud
The pale moon looks forth, with her strange tranquil gleam,
  Like a ghost in its shroud.

Her white smile the brown rolling river hath kissed;
  And I lift my sad eyes
To see her sail past through a rift in the mist
  That is veiling the skies.

And I think of the rest, in the dark waters near,
  To its stony bed given;
And I think of that light shining gentle and clear;—
  There is rest, too, in Heaven!

Till, the wild storm subsiding, forth comes by the moon
  One uprising star:
Is there rest? but the earth seems so near, as I swoon—
  And the Heavens so far!

                              Caroline Norton.

AMERICA TO GREAT BRITAIN.

ALL hail! thou noble land,
  Our fathers' native soil!
O stretch thy mighty hand,
  Gigantic grown by toil,
O'er the vast Atlantic wave to our shore;
  For thou, with magic might,
  Canst reach to where the light
  Of Phœbus travels bright
    The world o'er.

The genius of our clime,
  From his pine-embattled steep,
Shall hail the great sublime;
  While the Tritons of the deep
With their conchs the kindred league shall proclaim;
  Then let the world combine—
  O'er the main our naval line,
  Like the milky-way shall shine,
    Bright in fame!

Though ages long have passed
  Since our fathers left their home,
Their pilot in the blast,
  O'er untravelled seas to roam,—
Yet lives the blood of England in our veins!
  And shall we not proclaim
  That blood of honest fame,
  Which no tyranny can tame
    By its chains?

While the language free and bold
  Which the bard of Avon sung,
In which our Milton told
  How the vault of heaven rung,
When Satan, blasted, fell with his host;
  While this, with reverence meet,
  Ten thousand echoes greet,
  From rock to rock repeat
    Round our coast;

While the manners, while the arts,
  That mould a nation's soul,
Still cling around our hearts,
  Between let ocean roll,
Our joint communion breaking with the sun:
  Yet, still, from either beach,
  The voice of blood shall reach
  More audible than speech,
    "We are one!"

Washington Allston.

THE ARMADA.

ATTEND, all ye who list to hear our noble England's praise;
I sing of the thrice famous deeds she wrought in ancient days,
When that great fleet invincible against her bore, in vain
The richest spoils of Mexico, the stoutest hearts in Spain.

It was about the lovely close of a warm summer's day,
There came a gallant merchant-ship full sail to Plymouth
        bay;
The crew had seen Castile's black fleet, beyond Aurigny's
        isle,
At earliest twilight, on the waves lie heaving many a mile.
At sunrise she escaped their van, by God's especial grace;
And the tall Pinta, till the noon, had held her close in chase.
Forthwith a guard at every gun was placed along the wall;
The beacon blazed upon the roof of Edgecumbe's lofty hall;
Many a light fishing-bark put out to pry along the coast;
And with loose rein and bloody spur rode inland many a
        post.

With his white hair unbonneted, the stout old sheriff
        comes;
Behind him march the halberdiers; before him sound the
        drums:
The yeomen round the market cross make clear an ample
        space;
For there behoves him to set up the standard of Her Grace:
And haughtily the trumpets peal, and gaily dance the bells,
As slow upon the labouring wind the royal blazon swells.

Look how the Lion of the sea lifts up his ancient crown,
And underneath his deadly paw treads the gay lilies down!
So stalked he when he turned to flight, on that famed Picard
    field,
Bohemia's plume, and Genoa's bow, and Cæsar's eagle
    shield.
So glared he when at Agincourt in wrath he turned to bay,
And crushed and torn beneath his claws the princely
    hunters lay.
Ho! strike the flagstaff deep, Sir Knight: ho! scatter flowers,
    fair maids!
Ho, gunners! fire a loud salute: ho! gallants, draw your
    blades:
Thou sun, shine on her joyously; ye breezes, waft her wide;
Our glorious SEMPER EADEM! the banner of our pride.

    The fresh'ning breeze of eve unfurled that banner's massy
    fold—
The parting gleam of sunshine kissed that haughty scroll
    of gold:
Night sank upon the dusky beach, and on the purple sea;
Such night in England ne'er had been, nor e'er again
    shall be.
From Eddystone to Berwick bounds, from Lynn to Milford
    Bay,
That time of slumber was as bright and busy as the day;
For swift to east and swift to west the ghastly war-flame
    spread—
High on St. Michael's Mount it shone—it shone on Beachy
    Head:
Far o'er the deep the Spaniard saw, along each southern
    shire,
Cape beyond cape, in endless range, those twinkling points
    of fire.
The fisher left his skiff to rock on Tamar's glittering waves,
The rugged miners poured to war from Mendip's sunless
    caves;

O'er Longleat's towers, o'er Cranbourne's oaks, the fiery
    herald flew:
He roused the shepherds of Stonehenge—the rangers of
    Beaulieu.
Right sharp and quick the bells rang out all night from
    Bristol town,
And, ere the day, three hundred horse had met on Clifton
    Down.

    The sentinel on Whitehall gate looked forth into the night,
And saw, o'erhanging Richmond Hill that streak of blood-
    red light:
The bugle's note and cannon's roar, the death-like silence
    broke,
And with one start, and with one cry, the royal city woke.
At once on all her stately gates arose the answering
    fires;
At once the wild alarum clashed from all her reeling
    spires;
From all the batteries of the Tower pealed loud the voice
    of fear;
And all the thousand masts of Thames sent back a louder
    cheer:
And from the furthest wards was heard the rush of hurrying
    feet,
And the broad streams of pikes and flags rushed down
    each roaring street;
And broader still became the blaze, and louder still the din,
As fast from every village round the horse came spurring in;
And eastward straight from wild Blackheath the warlike
    errand went,
And roused in many an ancient hall the gallant squires of
    Kent:
Southward from Surrey's pleasant hills flew those bright
    couriers forth;
High on bleak Hampstead's swarthy moor they started for
    the north;

And on, and on, without a pause, untired they bounded still;
All night from tower to tower they sprang; they sprang
    from hill to hill;
Till the proud peak unfurled the flag o'er Darwin's rocky
    dales;
Till like volcanoes flared to heaven the stormy hills of
    Wales;
Till twelve fair counties saw the blaze on Malvern's lonely
    height;
Till streamed in crimson on the wind the Wrekin's crest
    of light;
Till broad and fierce the star came forth, on Ely's stately
    fane,
And tower and hamlet rose in arms o'er all the boundless
    plain;
Till Belvoir's lordly terraces the sign to Lincoln sent,
And Lincoln sped the message on o'er the wide vale of
    Trent:
Till Skiddaw saw the fire that burnt on Gaunt's embattled
    pile,
And the red glare on Skiddaw roused the burghers of
    Carlisle.

Lord Macaulay.

YE MARINERS OF ENGLAND.

YE mariners of England,
  That guard our native seas;
Whose flag has braved a thousand years
  The battle and the breeze!
Your glorious standard launch again
  To match another foe;
And sweep through the deep,
  While the stormy winds do blow;
While the battle rages loud and long,
  And the stormy winds do blow!

The spirits of your fathers
  Shall start from every wave;
For the deck it was their field of fame,
  And Ocean was their grave:
Where Blake and mighty Nelson fell,
  Your manly hearts shall glow,
As ye sweep through the deep,
  While the stormy winds do blow;
While the battle rages loud and long,
  And the stormy winds do blow!

Britannia needs no bulwarks,
  No towers along the steep;
Her march is o'er the mountain-waves,
  Her home is on the deep.

With thunders from her native oak
  She quells the floods below,
As they roar on the shore
  When the stormy winds do blow;
When the battle rages loud and long,
  And the stormy winds do blow!

The meteor flag of England
  Shall yet terrific burn;
Till danger's troubled night depart
  And the star of peace return.
Then, then, ye ocean-warriors!
  Our song and feast shall flow
To the fame of your name,
  When the storm has ceased to blow;
When the fiery fight is heard no more,
  And the storm has ceased to blow.

T. Campbell.

THE BATTLE OF THE BALTIC.

OF Nelson and the North
Sing the glorious day's renown,
When to battle fierce came forth
All the might of Denmark's crown,
And her arms along the deep proudly shone;
By each gun the lighted brand
In a bold determined hand,
And the Prince of all the land
Led them on.

Like leviathans afloat,
Lay their bulwarks on the brine;
While the sign of battle flew
On the lofty British line:

It was ten of April morn by the chime:
As they drifted on their path,
There was silence deep as death;
And the boldest held his breath
For a time.

But the might of England flush'd
To anticipate the scene;
And her van the fleeter rush'd
O'er the deadly space between.
"Hearts of oak!" our captains cried, when each gun
From its adamantine lips
Spread a dead-shade round the ships,
Like the hurricane eclipse
Of the sun.

Again! again! again!
And the havoc did not slack,
Till a feeble cheer the Dane
To our cheering sent us back;
Their shots along the deep slowly boom:—
Then ceased—and all is wail,
As they strike the shatter'd sail;
Or in conflagration pale
Light the gloom.

Out spoke the victor then
As he hail'd them o'er the wave,
"Ye are brothers! ye are men!
And we conquer but to save:
So peace instead of death let us bring;
But yield, proud foe, thy fleet
With the crews, at England's feet,
And make submission meet
To our King."   .

Then Denmark blest our chief
That he gave her wounds repose;
And the sounds of joy and grief
From her people wildly rose,
As death withdrew his shades from the day:
While the sun look'd smiling bright
O'er a wide and woeful sight,
Where the fires of funeral light
Died away.

Now joy, old England, raise!
For the tidings of thy might,
By the festal cities' blaze,
Whilst the wine cup shines in light;
And yet amidst that joy and uproar,
Let us think of them that sleep
Full many a fathom deep,
By thy wild and stormy steep,
Elsinore!

Brave hearts! to Britain's pride
Once so faithful and so true.
On the deck of fame that died,
With the gallant good Riou:
Soft sigh the winds of Heaven o'er their grave!
While the billow mournful rolls,
And the mermaid's song condoles,
Singing glory to the souls
Of the brave!

                                    T. Campbell.

THE CHARGE OF THE LIGHT BRIGADE.

(OCT. 25TH 1854.)

1.

HALF a league, half a league,
   Half a league onward,
All in the valley of Death
   Rode the six hundred.
"Forward, the Light Brigade!
"Charge for the guns!" he said:
Into the valley of Death
   Rode the six hundred.

2.

"Forward, the Light Brigade!"
Was there a man dismay'd?
Not tho' the soldier knew
   Someone had blunder'd:
Their's not to make reply,
Their's not to reason why,
Their's but to do and die:
Into the valley of Death
   Rode the six hundred.

3.

Cannon to right of them,
Cannon to left of them,
Cannon in front of them
   Volley'd and thunder'd;
Storm'd at with shot and shell,
Boldly they rode and well,
Into the jaws of Death,
Into the mouth of Hell
   Rode the six hundred.

4.

Flash'd all their sabres bare,
Flash'd as they turn'd in air,
Sabring the gunners there,
Charging an army, while
　All the world wonder'd:
Plung'd in the battery-smoke
Right through the line they broke;
Cossack and Russian
Reel'd from the sabre-stroke,
　Shatter'd and sunder'd.
Then they rode back, but not—
Not the six hundred.

5.

Cannon to right of them,
Cannon to left of them,
Cannon behind them
　Volley'd and thunder'd;
Storm'd at with shot and shell,
While horse and hero fell,
They that had fought so well
Came thro' the jaws of Death
Back from the mouth of Hell,
All that was left of them,
　Left of six hundred.

6.

When can their glory fade?
O the wild charge they made!
　All the world wonder'd.
Honour the charge they made!
Honour the Light Brigade,
　Noble six hundred!

A. Tennyson.

BARBARA FRITCHIE.

(AMERICAN CIVIL WAR; 1861—5.)

UP from the meadows rich with corn,
Clear from the cool September morn,
The clustered spires of Frederick stand,
Green-walled by the hills of Maryland.

Round about them orchards sweep,
Apple and peach-tree fruited deep;
Fair as a garden of the Lord
To the eyes of the famished rebel horde.

On that pleasant morn of the early fall,
When Lee marched over the mountain wall,
Over the mountains winding down,
Horse and foot, into Frederick town,

Forty flags with their silver stars,
Forty flags with their silver bars,
Flapped in the morning wind: the sun
Of noon looked down and saw not one.

Up rose old Barbara Fritchie then,
Bowed with her fourscore years and ten,
Bravest of all in Frederick town,
She took up the flag the men hauled down;

In her attic-window the staff she set,
To show that one heart was loyal yet.
Up the street came the rebel tread,
Stonewall Jackson riding ahead;

Under his slouched hat, left and right,
He glanced, the old flag met his sight.
"Halt!"—the dust-brown ranks stood fast;
"Fire!"—out blazed the rifle blast.

It shivered the window, pane and sash;
It rent the banner with seam and gash;
Quick, as it fell from the broken staff,
Dame Barbara snatched the silken scarf;

She leaned far out on the window sill
And shook it forth with a royal will.
"Shoot, if you must, this old grey head,
But spare your country's flag," she said.

A shade of sadness, a blush of shame,
Over the face of the leader came;
The noble nature within him stirred
To life, at that woman's deed and word.

"Who touches a hair of yon grey head,
Dies like a dog. March on!" he said.
All day long through Frederick street
Sounded the tread of marching feet;

All day long the free flag tossed
Over the heads of the rebel host;
Ever its torn folds rose and fell
On the loyal winds, that loved it well;

And through the hill-gaps sunset light
Shone over it with a warm good-night.
Barbara Fritchie's work is o'er,
And the rebel rides on his raid no more.

Honour to her! and let a tear
Fall, for her sake, on Stonewall's bier!

Over Barbara Fritchie's grave,
Flag of Freedom and Union, wave!

Peace, and order, and beauty draw
Round thy symbol of light and law;
And ever the stars above look down
On thy stars below, in Frederick town!

J. Greenleaf Whittier.

WHEN THE BOYS COME HOME.

(AMERICAN CIVIL WAR; 1861—5.)

THERE'S a happy time coming,
  When the boys come home.
There's a glorious day coming,
  When the boys come home.
We will end the dreadful story
Of this treason dark and gory
In a sunburst of glory,
  When the boys come home.

The day will seem brighter
  When the boys come home,
For our hearts will be lighter
  When the boys come home.
Wives and sweethearts will press them
In their arms, and caress them,
And pray God to bless them—
  When the boys come home.

The thinned ranks will be proudest,
  When the boys come home;
And their cheer will ring the loudest
  When the boys come home.

The full ranks will be shattered,
And the bright arms will be battered,
And the battle-standards tattered,
　　When the boys come home.

Their bayonets may be rusty,
　　When the boys come home,
And their uniforms dusty,
　　When the boys come home.
But all shall see the traces
Of battle's royal graces
In the brown and bearded faces,
　　When the boys come home.

Our love shall go to meet them,
　　When the boys come home;
To bless them and to greet them,
　　When the boys come home;
And the fame of their endeavour
Time and change shall not dissever
From the nation's heart for ever,
　　When the boys come home!

　　　　　　　　　Colonel John Hay.

THE MEN OF OLD.

I KNOW not that the men of old
Were better than men now,
Of heart more kind, of hand more bold,
Of more ingenuous brow:
I heed not those who pine for force
A ghost of Time to raise,
As if they thus could check the course
Of these appointed days.

Still it is true, and over true,
That I delight to close
This book of life self-wise and new,
And let my thoughts repose
On all that humble happiness
The world has since foregone—
The daylight of contentedness
That on those faces shone!

With rights, tho' not too closely scanned,
Enjoyed, as far as known—
With will by no reverse unmanned—
With pulse of even tone—
They from to-day and from to-night
Expected nothing more
Than yesterday and yesternight
Had proffered them before.

To them was life a simple art
Of duties to be done,
A game where each man took his part,
A race where all must run;
A battle whose great scheme and scope
They little cared to know,
Content, as men at arms, to cope
Each with his fronting foe.

Man *now* his Virtue's diadem
Puts on and proudly wears;
Great thoughts, great feelings, came to them
Like instincts, unawares:
Blending their souls' sublimest needs
With tasks of every day,
They went about their gravest deeds
As noble boys at play.

And what if Nature's fearful wound
They did not probe and bare,
For that their spirits never swooned
To watch the misery there—
For that their love but flowed more fast,
Their charities more free,
Not conscious what mere drops they cast
Into the evil sea.

A man's best things are nearest him,
Lie close about his feet,
It is the distant and the dim
That we are sick to greet:
For flowers that grow our hands beneath
We struggle and aspire—
Our hearts must die, except they breathe
The air of fresh Desire.

Yet, brothers, who up Reason's hill
Advance with hopeful cheer—
O! loiter not, those heights are chill,
As chill as they are clear;
And still restrain your haughty gaze,
The loftier that ye go,
Remembering distance leaves a haze
On all that lies below.

Lord Houghton.

THE PRIDE OF WORTH.

Is there, for honest poverty,
  That hangs his head, and a' that?
The coward-slave, we pass him by,
  And dare be poor for a' that!
    For a' that, and a' that,
      Our toil's obscure, and a' that;
      The rank is but the guinea stamp;
      The man's the gowd for a' that.

What tho' on hamely fare we dine,
  Wear hodden-grey, and a' that;
Gie fools their silks, and knaves their wine,
  A man's a man, for a' that.
    For a' that, and a' that,
      Their tinsel show, and a' that:
      The honest man, tho' ne'er sae poor,
      Is King o' men for a' that.

Ye see yon birkie, ca'd a lord,
  Wha struts, and stares, and a' that;
Tho' hundreds worship at his word,
  He's but a coof for a' that:
    For a' that, and a' that,
      His riband, star, and a' that,
      The man, of independent mind,
      He looks and laughs at a' that.

A king can mak a belted knight,
  A marquis, duke, and a' that;
But an honest man's aboon his might,
  Guid faith, he maunna fa' that!

13*

For a' that, and a' that,
  Their dignities, and a' that,
The pith o' sense, and pride o' worth,
  Are higher ranks than a' that.

Then let us pray that come it may,
  As come it will for a' that,
That sense and worth, o'er a' the earth,
  May bear the gree, and a' that;
  For a' that, and a' that,
    It's coming yet, for a' that;
  That man to man, the warld o'er,
    Shall brothers be for a' that.

R. Burns.

GOLD.

GOLD! Gold! Gold! Gold!
Bright and yellow, hard and cold,
Molten, graven, hammer'd and roll'd;
Heavy to get and light to hold;
Hoarded, barter'd, bought, and sold,
Stolen, borrow'd, squander'd, doled;
Spurn'd by the young, but hugg'd by the old
To the very verge of the churchyard mould;
Price of many a crime untold;
Gold! Gold! Gold! Gold!
Good or bad a thousand-fold!
  How widely its agencies vary—
To save—to ruin—to curse—to bless—
As even its minted coins express,
Now stamp'd with the image of Good Queen Bess,
  And now of a Bloody Mary.

T. Hood.

THE WORLDLINESS OF TO-DAY.

THE world is too much with us; late and soon,
Getting and spending, we lay waste our powers:
Little we see in Nature that is ours;
We have given our hearts away, a sordid boon!
This sea that bares her bosom to the moon;
The winds that will be howling at all hours
And are up-gathered now like sleeping flowers;
For this, for everything, we are out of tune;
It moves us not.   Great God! I'd rather be
A pagan suckled in a creed outworn,
So might I, standing on this pleasant lea,
Have glimpses that would make me less forlorn —
Have sight of Proteus coming from the sea,
Or hear old Triton blow his wreathèd horn.

W. Wordsworth.

THE LATEST DECALOGUE.

THOU shalt have one God only; who
Would be at the expense of two?
No graven images may be
Worshipped—except the currency.
Swear not at all—for, for thy curse
Thine enemy is none the worse.
At church on Sunday to attend
Will serve to keep the world thy friend.
Honour thy parents—that is, all
From whom advancement may befall.
Thou shalt not kill—but need'st not strive
Officiously to keep alive.
Do not adultery commit;
Advantage rarely comes of it.
Thou shalt not steal—an empty feat
When 'tis so lucrative to cheat.
Bear not false witness; let the lie
Have time on its own wings to fly.
Thou shalt not covet; but tradition
Approves all forms of competition.

Arthur Hugh Clough.

SAINT BRANDAN.

SAINT Brandan sails the northern main;
The brotherhoods of saints are glad.
He greets them once, he sails again.
So late!—such storms!—The Saint is mad!

He heard across the howling seas
Chime convent bells on wintry nights,
He saw on spray-swept Hebrides
Twinkle the monastery lights;

But north, still north, Saint Brandan steer'd;
And now no bells, no convents more!
The hurtling Polar lights are near'd,
The sea without a human shore.

At last—(it was the Christmas night,
Stars shone after a day of storm)—
He sees float past an iceberg white,
And on it—Christ!—a living form!

That furtive mien, that scowling eye,
Of hair that red and tufted fell——
It is—Oh, where shall Brandan fly?—
The traitor Judas, out of hell!

Palsied with terror, Brandan sate;
The moon was bright, the iceberg near.
He hears a voice sigh humbly: "Wait!
By high permission I am here.

"One moment wait, thou holy man!
On earth my crime, my death, they knew;
My name is under all men's ban;
Ah, tell them of my respite too!

"Tell them, one blessed Christmas night—
(It was the first after I came,
Breathing self-murder, frenzy, spite,
To rue my guilt in endless flame)—

"I felt, as I in torment lay
'Mid the souls plagued by heavenly power,
An angel touch mine arm, and say:
Go hence, and cool thyself an hour!

"'Ah, whence this mercy, Lord?' I said.
The Leper recollect, said he,
Who ask'd the passers-by for aid,
In Joppa, and thy charity.

"Then I remember'd how I went,
In Joppa, through the public street,
One morn, when the sirocco spent
Its storms of dust, with burning heat;

"And in the street a Leper sate,
Shivering with fever, naked, old;
Sand raked his sores from heel to pate,
The hot wind fever'd him five-fold.

"He gazed upon me as I pass'd,
  And murmur'd: *Help me, or I die!*—
To the poor wretch my cloak I cast,
  Saw him look eased, and hurried by.

"Oh, Brandan, think what grace divine,
  What blessing must full goodness shower,
If fragment of it small, like mine,
  Hath such inestimable power!

"Well-fed, well-clothed, well-friended, I
  Did that chance act of good, that one!
Then went my way to kill and lie—
  Forgot my good as soon as done.

"That germ of kindness, in the womb
  Of mercy caught, did not expire;
Outlives my guilt, outlives my doom,
  And friends me in the pit of fire.

"Once every year, when carols wake,
  On earth, the Christmas night's repose,
Arising from the sinners' lake,
  I journey to these healing snows.

"I stanch with ice my burning breast,
  With silence balm my whirling brain.
O Brandan! to this hour of rest,
  That Joppan leper's ease was pain!"——

Tears started to Saint Brandan's eyes;
He bow'd his head; he breathed a prayer.
When he look'd up—tenantless lies
The iceberg in the frosty air!

Matthew Arnold.

ABOU BEN ADHEM AND THE ANGEL.

ABOU BEN ADHEM (may his tribe increase!)
Awoke one night from a deep dream of peace,
And saw, within the moonlight in his room,
Making it rich, and like a lily in bloom,
An angel, writing in a book of gold:—
Exceeding peace had made Ben Adhem bold,
And to the presence in the room he said,
"What writest thou?"—The vision raised its head,
And, with a look made of all sweet accord,
Answered, "The names of those who love the Lord."
"And is mine one?" said Abou. "Nay, not so,"
Replied the angel. Abou spoke more low,
But cheerly still; and said, "I pray thee, then,
Write me as one that loves his fellow-men."

The angel wrote, and vanished. The next night
It came again with a great wakening light,
And showed the names whom love of God had blessed,
And lo! Ben Adhem's name led all the rest.

Leigh Hunt.

THE OLD MAN DREAMS.

OH, for one hour of youthful joy!
  Give back my twentieth spring!
I'd rather laugh a bright-haired boy
  Than reign a gray-beard king!

Off with the wrinkled spoils of age!
  Away with learning's crown!
Tear out life's wisdom-written page,
  And dash its trophies down!

One moment let my life-blood stream
  From boyhood's fount of flame!
Give me one giddy, reeling dream
  Of life all love and fame!

—My listening angel heard the prayer,
  And, calmly smiling, said
"If I but touch thy silvered hair,
  Thy hasty wish hath sped.

But is there nothing in thy track
  To bid thee fondly stay,
While the swift seasons hurry back
  To find the wished-for day?"

—Ah, truest soul of womankind!
  Without thee, what were life?
One bliss I cannot leave behind:
  I'll take—my—precious wife!

—The angel took a sapphire pen
  And wrote in rainbow dew,
"The man would be a boy again,
  And be a husband too!"

—"And is there nothing yet unsaid
  Before the change appears?
Remember, all their gifts have fled
  With those dissolving years!"

Why, yes; for memory would recall
  My fond paternal joys;
I could not bear to leave them all;
  I'll take—my girl—and—boys!

The smiling angel dropped his pen,—
  "Why, this will never do;
The man would be a boy again,
  And be a father too!"

And so I laughed:—my laughter woke
  The household with its noise,—
And wrote my dream, when morning broke,
  To please the gray-haired boys.

Oliver Wendell Holmes.

SAND OF THE DESERT IN AN HOURGLASS.

A HANDFUL of red sand, from the hot clime
    Of Arab deserts brought,
Within this glass becomes the spy of Time,
    The minister of Thought.

How many weary centuries has it been
    About those deserts blown!
How many strange vicissitudes has seen,
    How many histories known!

Perhaps the camels of the Ishmaelite
    Trampled and passed it o'er,
When into Egypt from the patriarch's sight
    His favourite son they bore.

Perhaps the feet of Moses, burnt and bare,
    Crushed it beneath their tread;
Or Pharaoh's flashing wheels into the air
    Scattered it as they sped;

Or Mary, with the Christ of Nazareth
    Held close in her caress,
Whose pilgrimage of hope and love and faith
    Illumed the wilderness;

Or anchorites beneath Engaddi's palms
    Pacing the Dead Sea beach,
And singing slow their old Armenian psalms
    In half-articulate speech;

Or caravans, that from Bassora's gate
  With westward steps depart;
Or Mecca's pilgrims, confident of Fate,
   And resolute in heart!

These have passed over it, or may have passed!
  Now, in this crystal tower
Imprisoned by some curious hand at last,
  It counts the passing hour.

And as I gaze, these narrow walls expand;—
  Before my dreamy eye
Stretches the desert with its shifting sand,
  Its unimpeded sky.

And borne aloft by the sustaining blast,
  This little golden thread
Dilates into a column high and vast,
  A form of fear and dread.

And onward, and across the setting sun,
  Across the boundless plain,
The column and its broader shadow run,
  Till thought pursues in vain.

The vision vanishes! These walls again
  Shut out the lurid sun,
Shut out the hot immeasurable plain;
  The half-hour's sand is run!

H. W. Longfellow.

THE KNIGHT'S TOMB.

WHERE is the grave of Sir Arthur O'Kellyn?
Where may the grave of that good man be?—
By the side of a spring, on the breast of Helvellyn,
Under the twigs of a young birch tree!
The oak that in summer was sweet to hear,
And rustled its leaves in the fall of the year,
And whistled and roared in the winter alone,
Is gone,—and the birch in its stead is grown.—
The Knight's bones are dust,
And his good sword rust;—
His soul is with the saints, I trust.

S. T. Coleridge.

THE ISLE.

THERE was a little lawny islet,
By anemone and violet,
  Like mosaic, paven:
And its roof was flowers and leaves
Which the summer's breath enweaves,

Where nor sun nor showers nor breeze
Pierce the pines and tallest trees,—
  Each a gem engraven:
Girt by many an azure wave
With which the clouds and mountains pave
  A lake's blue chasm.

P. B. Shelley.

CANZONET.

DEAR is my little native vale,
The ring-dove builds and murmurs there;
Close by my cot she tells her tale
To every passing villager.
The squirrel leaps from tree to tree
And shells his nuts at liberty.

In orange-groves and myrtle-bow'rs,
That breathe a gale of fragrance round,
I charm the fairy-footed hours
With my loved lute's romantic sound;
Or crowns of living laurel weave,
For those that win the race at eve.

The shepherd's horn at break of day,
The ballet danced in twilight glade,
The canzonet and roundelay
Sung in the silent green-wood shade;
These simple joys, that never fail,
Shall bind me to my native vale.

S. Rogers.

THE MORNING-LAND.

KNOW ye the land where the cypress and myrtle
  Are emblems of deeds that are done in their clime,
Where the rage of the vulture, the love of the turtle,
  Now melt into sorrow, now madden to crime?
Know ye the land of the cedar and vine,
Where the flowers ever blossom, the beams ever shine;
Where the light wings of Zephyr, oppressed with perfume,
Wax faint o'er the gardens of Gúl in her bloom?
Where the citron and olive are fairest of fruit,
And the voice of the nightingale never is mute,
Where the tints of the earth, and the hues of the sky,
In colour though varied, in beauty may vie,
And the purple of Ocean is deepest in dye;
Where the virgins are soft as the roses they twine,
And all, save the spirit of man, is divine?
'Tis the clime of the East; 'tis the land of the Sun—
Can he smile on such deeds as his children have done?
Oh! wild as the accents of lovers' farewell
Are the hearts which they bear, and the tales which they tell.

Lord Byron.

LOVE'S PHILOSOPHY.

THE fountains mingle with the river
And the rivers with the ocean,
The winds of heaven mix for ever
With a sweet emotion;
Nothing in the world is single,
All things by a law divine
In one another's being mingle—
   Why not I with thine?

See, the mountains kiss high heaven
And the waves clasp one another;
No sister-flower would be forgiven
If it disdain'd its brother:
And the sunlight clasps the earth,
And the moonbeams kiss the sea—
What are all these kissings worth,
   If thou kiss not me?

                          P. B. Shelley.

LOVE'S EXAMPLES.

THE violet loves a sunny bank,
  The cowslip loves the lea,
The scarlet creeper loves the elm;
  But I love—thee!

The sunshine kisses mount and vale,
  The stars they kiss the sea,
The west winds kiss the clover blooms;
  But I kiss—thee!

The oriole weds his mottled mate,
  The lily's bride o' the bee,
Heaven's marriage-ring is round the earth;
  Shall I wed—thee?

J. Bayard Taylor.

JENNY'S KISS.

JENNY kissed me when we met,
  Jumping from the chair she sat in;
Time, you thief! who love to get
  Sweets into your list, put that in.
Say I'm weary, say I'm sad,
  Say that health and wealth have missed me,
Say I'm growing dull, but add—
  Jenny kissed me!

L. Hunt.

14*

SWEET PERIL.

ALAS! how easily things go wrong—
A sigh too much, or a kiss too long,
And there follows a mist and a weeping rain,
And life is never the same again.

Alas! how hardly things go right—
'Tis hard to watch in a summer night,
For the sigh will come, and the kiss will stay,
And the summer night is a winter day.

George Macdonald.

FLOWERS.

I WILL not have the maid Clytie
Whose head is turn'd by the sun;
The tulip is a courtly quean,
Whom, therefore, I will shun;
The cowslip is a country wench,
The violet is a nun;—
But I will woo the dainty rose,
The queen of every one.

The pea is but a wanton witch,
In too much haste to wed,
And clasps her rings on every hand;
The wolfsbane I should dread;
Nor will I dreary rosemarye,
That always mourns the dead;—
But I will woo the dainty rose,
With her cheeks of tender red.

The lily is all in white, like a saint,
And so is no mate for me—
And the daisy's cheek is tipp'd with a blush,
She is of such low degree;
Jasmine is sweet, and has many loves,
And the broom's betroth'd to the bee;—
But I will plight with the dainty rose,
For fairest of all is she.

T. Hood.

THE QUEEN'S RIDE.

'TIS that fair time of year,
 Lady mine!
When stately Guinevere,
In her sea-green robe and hood,
Went a-riding through the wood,
 Lady mine!

And as the Queen did ride,
 Lady mine!
Sir Launcelot at her side
Laughed and chatted, bending over,
Half her friend and all her lover,—
 Lady mine!

And as they rode along,
 Lady mine!
The throstle gave them song,
And the buds peeped through the grass
To see youth and beauty pass,
 Lady mine!

And on, through deathless time,
    Lady mine!
These lovers in their prime,
(Two fairy ghosts together!)
Ride, with sea-green robe and feather,
    Lady mine!

And so we two will ride,
    Lady mine!
At your pleasure, side by side,
Laugh and chat,—I bending over,
Half your friend and all your lover,
    Lady mine!

But if you like not this
    Lady mine!
And take my love amiss,
Then I'll ride unto the end,
Half your lover, all your friend,—
    Lady mine!

So come which way you will,
    Lady mine!
Vale, upland, plain, and hill
Wait your coming. For one day
Loose the bridle, and away!
    Lady mine!

Thomas Bailey Aldrich.

LETTICE WHITE.

My neighbour White—we met to-day—
He always had a cheerful way,
  As if he breathed at ease;
My neighbour White lives down the glade,
And I live higher, in the shade
  Of my old walnut trees.

So many lads and lasses small,
To feed them all, to clothe them all,
  Must surely tax his wit;
I see his thatch when I look out,
His branching roses creep about,
  And vines half smother it.

There white-haired urchins climb his eaves
And little watch-fires heap with leaves,
  And milky filberts hoard;
And there his oldest daughter stands
With downcast eyes and skilful hands
  Before her ironing-board.

She comforts all her mother's days,
And with her sweet obedient ways
  She makes her labour light;
So sweet to hear, so fair to see!
O, she is much too good for me,
  That lovely Lettice White!

'T is hard to feel oneself a fool!
With that same lass I went to school—
   I then was great and wise;
She read upon an easier book,
And I—I never cared to look
   Into her shy blue eyes.

And now I know they must be there,
Sweet eyes, behind those lashes fair
   That will not raise their rim:
If maids be shy, he cures who can;
But if a man be shy—a man—
   Why then the worse for him;

My mother cries, "For such a lad
A wife is easy to be had
   And always to be found;
A finer scholar scarce can be,
And for a foot and leg," says she,
   "He beats the country round!

"My handsome boy must stoop his head
   To clear her door whom he would wed."
   Weak praise, but fondly sung!
"O mother! scholars sometimes fail—
   And what can foot and leg avail
   To him that wants a tongue?"

When by her ironing-board I sit,
Her little sisters round me flit,
   And bring me forth their store;
Dark cluster grapes of dusty blue,
And small sweet apples bright of hue
   And crimson to the core.

But she abideth silent, fair,
All shaded by her flaxen hair
  The blushes come and go;
I look, and I no more can speak
Than the red sun that on her cheek
  Smiles as he lieth low.

Sometimes the roses by the latch
Or scarlet vine-leaves from her thatch
  Come sailing down like birds;
When from their drifts her board I clear,
She thanks me, but I scarce can hear
  The shyly uttered words.

Oft have I wooed sweet Lettice White
By daylight and by candlelight
  When we two were apart.
Some better day come on apace,
And let me tell her face to face,
  "Maiden, thou hast my heart."

How gently rock yon poplars high
Against the reach of primrose sky
  With heaven's pale candles stored!
She sees them all, sweet Lettice White;
I'll e'en go sit again to-night
  Beside her ironing-board!

J. Ingelow.

APPRENTICED.

(OLD STYLE.)

"COME out and hear the waters shoot, the owlet hoot, the
    owlet hoot;
  Yon crescent moon, a golden boat, hangs dim behind the
    tree, O!
The dropping thorn makes white the grass, O sweetest lass,
    and sweetest lass;
  Come out and smell the ricks of hay adown the croft with
    me, O!"

"My granny nods before her wheel, and drops her reel, and
    drops her reel;
  My father with his crony talks as gay as gay can be, O!
But all the milk is yet to skim, ere light wax dim, ere light
    wax dim;
  How can I step adown the croft, my 'prentice lad, with
    thee, O?"

"And must ye bide, yet waiting's long, and love is strong,
    and love is strong;
  And O! had I but served the time that takes so long to
    flee, O!
And thou, my lass, by morning's light, wast all in white,
    wast all in white;
  And parson stood within the rails, a-marrying me and
    thee, O!"

J. Ingelow.

THE LONG WHITE SEAM.

As I came round the harbour buoy,
  The lights began to gleam,
No wave the land-locked harbour stirred,
  The crags were white as cream;
And I marked my love by candlelight
  Sewing her long white seam.
    It's aye sewing ashore, my dear,
      Watch and steer at sea,
    It's reef and furl, and haul the line,
      Set sail and think of thee.

I climbed to reach her cottage door;
  O sweetly my love sings;
Like a shaft of light her voice breaks forth,
  My soul to meet it springs,
As the shining water leaped of old
  When stirred by angel wings.
    Aye longing to list anew,
      Awake and in my dream,
    But never a song she sang like this,
      Sewing her long white seam.

Fair fall the lights, the harbour lights,
  That brought me in to thee,
And peace drop down on that low roof,
  For the sight that I did see,
And the voice, my dear, that rang so clear,
  All for the love of me.
    For O, for O, with brows bent low,
      By the flickering candle's gleam,
    Her wedding gown it was she wrought,
      Sewing the long white seam.

J. Ingelow.

THE SOLITARY REAPER.

BEHOLD her, single in the field,
Yon solitary Highland Lass!
Reaping and singing by herself;
Stop here, or gently pass!
Alone she cuts and binds the grain,
And sings a melancholy strain;
O listen! for the Vale profound
Is overflowing with the sound.

No Nightingale did ever chaunt
More welcome notes to weary bands
Of travellers in some shady haunt,
Among Arabian sands:
A voice so thrilling ne'er was heard
In spring-time from the Cuckoo-bird,
Breaking the silence of the seas
Among the farthest Hebrides.

Will no one tell me what she sings?—
Perhaps the plaintive numbers flow
For old, unhappy, far-off things,
And battles long ago:
Or is it some more humble lay,
Familiar matter of to-day?
Some natural sorrow, loss, or pain,
That has been, and may be again?

Whate'er the theme, the Maiden sang
As if her song could have no ending;
I saw her singing at her work,
And o'er the sickle bending;—
I listened, motionless and still;
And, as I mounted up the hill,
The music in my heart I bore,
Long after it was heard no more.

W. Wordsworth.

TO A LADY, WITH A GUITAR.

ARIEL to Miranda:—Take
This slave of music, for the sake
Of him, who is the slave of thee;
And teach it all the harmony
In which thou canst, and only thou,
Make the delighted spirit glow,
Till joy denies itself again,
And, too intense, is turned to pain.
For, by permission and command
Of thine own Prince Ferdinand,
Poor Ariel sends this silent token
Of more than ever can be spoken;
Your guardian spirit Ariel, who
From life to life must still pursue
Your happiness, for thus alone
Can Ariel ever find his own.
From Prospero's enchanted cell,
As the mighty verses tell,
To the throne of Naples he
Lit you o'er the trackless sea,
Flitting on, your prow before,
Like a living meteor.

When you die, the silent Moon
In her interlunar swoon
Is not sadder in her cell
Than deserted Ariel.
When you live again on earth,—
Like an unseen star of birth,
Ariel guides you o'er the sea
Of life from your nativity.
Many changes have been run
Since Ferdinand and you begun
Your course of love, and Ariel still
Has tracked your steps and served your will.
Now, in humbler happier lot,
This is all remembered not;
And now, alas! the poor Sprite is
Imprisoned for some fault of his
In a body like a grave:
From you he only dares to crave,
For his service and his sorrow,
A smile to-day, a song to-morrow.

The artist who this idol wrought,
To echo all harmonious thought,
Felled a tree while on the steep
The woods were in their winter sleep,
Rocked in that repose divine
On the wind-swept Apennine,
And dreaming, some of Autumn past,
And some of Spring approaching fast,
And some of April buds and showers,
And some of songs in July bowers,
And all of love.   And so this tree—
Oh that such our death may be!—
Died in sleep, and felt no pain,
To live in happier form again:
From which, beneath heaven's fairest star,
The artist wrought this loved Guitar,

And taught it justly to reply,
To all who question skilfully,
In language gentle as thine own;
Whispering in enamoured tone
Sweet oracles of woods and dells,
And summer winds in sylvan cells.
For it had learnt all harmonies
Of the plains and of the skies,
Of the forests and the mountains,
And the many-voicèd fountains;
The clearest echoes of the hills,
The softest notes of falling rills,
The melodies of birds and bees,
The murmuring of summer seas,
And pattering rain, and breathing dew,
And airs of evening; and it knew
That seldom-heard mysterious sound
Which, driven on its diurnal round,
As it floats through boundless day,
Our world enkindles on its way:
—All this it knows, but will not tell
To those who cannot question well
The spirit that inhabits it;
It talks according to the wit
Of its companions; and no more
Is heard than has been felt before
By those who tempt it to betray
These secrets of an elder day.
But, sweetly as its answers will
Flatter hands of perfect skill,
It keeps its highest holiest tone
For one beloved Friend alone.

P. B. Shelley.

CARILLON.

In the ancient town of Bruges,
In the quaint old Flemish city,
As the evening shades descended,
Low and loud and sweetly blended,
Low at times and loud at times
And changing like a poet's rhymes,
Rang the beautiful wild chimes
From the belfry in the market
Of the ancient town of Bruges.

Then, with deep sonorous clangor
Calmly answering their sweet anger,
When the wrangling bells had ended,
Slowly struck the clock eleven,
And, from out the silent heaven,
Silence on the town descended.
Silence, silence everywhere,
On the earth and in the air,
Save that footsteps here and there
Of some burgher home returning,
By the street lamps faintly burning,
For a moment woke the echoes
Of the ancient town of Bruges.

But amid my broken slumbers
Still I heard those magic numbers,
As they loud proclaimed the flight
And stolen marches of the night;
Till their chimes in sweet collision
Mingled with each wandering vision,

Mingled with the fortune-telling
Gipsy-bands of dreams and fancies,
Which amid the waste expanses
Of the silent land of trances
Have their solitary dwelling.
All else seemed asleep in Bruges,
In the quaint old Flemish city.

And I thought how like these chimes
Are the poet's airy rhymes,
All his rhymes and roundelays,
His conceits, and songs, and ditties,
From the belfry of his brain,
Scattered downward, though in vain,
On the roofs and stones of cities!
For by night the drowsy ear
Under its curtains cannot hear,
And by day men go their ways,
Hearing the music as they pass,
But deeming it no more, alas!
Than the hollow sound of brass.

Yet perchance a sleepless wight,
Lodging at some humble inn
In the narrow lanes of life,
When the dusk and hush of night
Shut out the incessant din
Of daylight and its toil and strife,
May listen with a calm delight
To the poet's melodies,
Till he hears, or dreams he hears,
Intermingled with the song,
Thoughts that he has cherished long;
Hears amid the chime and singing
The bells of his own village ringing,
And wakes, and finds his slumbrous eyes
Wet with most delicious tears.

Thus dreamed I, as by night I lay
In Bruges, at the Fleur-de-Blé,
Listening with a wild delight
To the chimes that, through the night,
Rang their changes from the Belfry
Of that quaint old Flemish city.

H. W. Longfellow.

THE BELFRY OF BRUGES.

IN the market-place of Bruges stands the belfry old and
    brown;
Thrice consumed and thrice rebuilded, still it watches o'er
    the town.

As the summer morn was breaking, on that lofty tower I
    stood,
And the world threw off the darkness, like the weeds of
    widowhood.

Thick with towns and hamlets studded, and with streams
    and vapours gray,
Like a shield embossed with silver, round and vast the
    landscape lay.

At my feet the city slumbered. From its chimneys, here
    and there,
Wreaths of snow-white smoke, ascending, vanished, ghost-
    like, into air.

Not a sound rose from the city at that early morning
    hour,
But I heard a heart of iron beating in the ancient tower.

From their nests beneath the rafters sang the swallows wild
  and high;
And the world, beneath me sleeping, seemed more distant
  than the sky.

Then, most musical and solemn, bringing back the olden
  times,
With their strange, unearthly changes rang the melancholy
  chimes,

Like the psalms from some old cloister, when the nuns sing
  in the choir;
And the great bell tolled among them, like the chanting of
  a friar.

Visions of the days departed, shadowy phantoms filled my
  brain;
They who live in history only seemed to walk the earth
  again:

All the Foresters of Flanders,—mighty Baldwin Bras de
  Fer,
.Lyderick du Bucq and Cressy, Philip, Guy de Dampierre.

I beheld the pageants splendid, that adorned those days of
  old;
Stately dames, like queens attended, knights who bore the
  Fleece of Gold;

Lombard and Venetian merchants with deep-laden argosies;
Ministers from twenty nations; more than royal pomp and
  ease.

I beheld proud Maximilian, kneeling humbly on the
  ground:
I beheld the gentle Mary, hunting with her hawk and
  hound;

.15*

And her lighted bridal-chamber, where a duke slept with
    the queen;
And the armèd guard around them, and the sword un-
    sheathed between.

I beheld the Flemish weavers, with Namur and Juliers bold,
Marching homeward from the bloody battle of the Spurs of
    Gold;

Saw the fight at Minnewater, saw the White Hoods moving
    west;
Saw great Artevelde victorious scale the Golden Dragon's
    nest.

And again the whiskered Spaniard all the land with terror
    smote;
And again the wild alarum sounded from the tocsin's
    throat;

Till the bell of Ghent responded o'er lagoon and dyke of
    sand,
"I am Roland! I am Roland! there is victory in the land!"

Then the sound of drums aroused me. The awakened city's
    roar
Chased the phantoms I had summoned back into their
    graves once more.

Hours had passed away like minutes; and, before I was
    aware,
Lo! the shadow of the belfry crossed the sun-illumined
    square.

H. W. Longfellow.

THE BELLS.

HEAR the sledges with the bells—
    Silver bells!
What a world of merriment their melody foretells!
   How they tinkle, tinkle, tinkle,
  In the icy air of night!
   While the stars that oversprinkle
   All the heavens, seem to twinkle
  With a crystalline delight;
      Keeping time, time, time,
    In a sort of Runic rhyme,
To the tintinabulation that so musically swells
From the bells, bells, bells, bells,
     Bells, bells, bells—
From the jingling and the tinkling of the bells.

   Hear the mellow wedding bells,
    Golden bells!
What a world of happiness their harmony foretells!
   Through the balmy air of night
   How they ring out their delight!
    From the molten-golden notes,
     And all in tune,
   What a liquid ditty floats
To the turtle-dove that listens, while she gloats
    On the moon!
  Oh, from out the sounding cells,
What a gush of euphony voluminously wells!
    How it swells;
    How it dwells

On the Future! how it tells
Of the rapture that impels
To the swinging and the ringing
Of the bells, bells, bells,
Of the bells, bells, bells, bells,
Bells, bells, bells—
To the rhyming and the chiming of the bells!

Hear the loud alarum bells—
Brazen bells!
What a tale of terror, now, their turbulency tells!
In the startled ear of night
How they scream out their affright!
Too much horrified to speak,
They can only shriek, shriek,
Out of tune,
In a clamorous appealing to the mercy of the fire,
In a mad expostulation with the deaf and frantic fire
Leaping higher, higher, higher,
With a desperate desire,
And a resolute endeavour
Now—now to sit, or never,
By the side of the pale-faced moon.
Oh, the bells, bells, bells!
What a tale their terror tells
Of Despair!
How they clang, and clash, and roar!
What a horror they outpour
On the bosom of the palpitating air!
Yet the ear it fully knows,
By the twanging,
And the clanging,
How the danger ebbs and flows;
Yet the ear distinctly tells,
In the jangling,
And the wrangling,
How the danger sinks and swells,

By the sinking or the swelling in the anger of the bells—
　　Of the bells—
　Of the bells, bells, bells, bells,
　　Bells, bells, bells—
In the clamour and the clangour of the bells!

　　Hear the tolling of the bells—
　　　Iron bells!
What a world of solemn thought their monody compels!
　　In the silence of the night,
　　How we shiver with affright
　At the melancholy menace of their tone!
　　For every sound that floats
　　From the rust within their throats
　　　Is a groan.
　And the people—ah, the people—
　They that dwell up in the steeple,
　　　All alone,
　And who tolling, tolling, tolling,
　　In that muffled monotone,
　Feel a glory in so rolling
　　On the human heart a stone—
They are neither man nor woman—
They are neither brute nor human—
　　　They are Ghouls:
And their king it is who tolls;
And he rolls, rolls, rolls,
　　　Rolls
　　A pæan from the bells!
And his merry bosom swells
　　With the pæan of the bells!
And he dances, and he yells;
Keeping time, time, time,
In a sort of Runic rhyme,
　　To the pæan of the bells—
　　　. Of the bells:

Keeping time, time, time,
In a sort of Runic rhyme,
   To the throbbing of the bells—
Of the bells, bells, bells—
   To the sobbing of the bells;
Keeping time, time, time,
   As he knells, knells, knells,
In a happy Runic rhyme,
   To the rolling of the bells—
Of the bells, bells, bells—
   To the tolling of the bells—
Of the bells, bells, bells, bells—
   Bells, bells, bells—
To the moaning and the groaning of the bells.

E. A. Poe.

THE HIGH TIDE ON THE COAST
OF LINCOLNSHIRE

(1571.)

THE old mayor climbed the belfry tower,
   The ringers ran by two, by three;
"Pull, if ye never pulled before;
   Good ringers, pull your best," quoth he,
"Play uppe, play uppe, O Boston bells!
Ply all your changes, all your swells,
   Play uppe 'The Brides of Enderby,'"

Men say it was a stolen tyde—
   The Lord that sent it, He knows all;
But in myne ears doth still abide
   The message that the bells let fall:
And there was nought of strange, beside
The flights of mews and peewits pied
   By millions crouched on the old sea wall.

I sat and spun within the doore,
  My thread brake off, I raised myne eyes;
The level sun, like ruddy ore,
  Lay sinking in the barren skies
And dark against day's golden death
She moved where Lindis wandereth,
My sonne's faire wife, Elizabeth.

"Cusha! Cusha! Cusha!" calling,
  Ere the early dews were falling,
Farre away I heard her song.
"Cusha! Cusha!" all along;
  Where the reedy Lindis floweth,
    Floweth, floweth,
From the meads where melick groweth
Faintly came her milking song—

"Cusha! Cusha! Cusha!" calling,
"For the dews will soone be falling;
 Leave your meadow grasses mellow,
    Mellow, mellow;
Quit your cowslips, cowslips yellow;
Come uppe Whitefoot, come uppe Lightfoot;
Quit the stalks of parsley hollow,
  Hollow, hollow;
Come uppe Jetty, rise and follow,
From the clovers lift your head;
Come uppe Whitefoot, come uppe Lightfoot,
Come uppe Jetty, rise and follow,
Jetty, to the milking shed."

If it be long, ay, long ago,
  When I beginne to think howe long,
Againe I hear the Lindis flow,
  Swift as an arrowe, sharpe and strong;
And all the aire, it seemeth mee,

Bin full of floating bells (sayth shee),
That ring the tune of Enderby.

Alle fresh the level pasture lay,
　And not a shadowe mote be seene,
Save where full fyve good miles away
　The steeple towered from out the greene;
And lo! the great bell farre and wide
Was heard in all the country side
That Saturday at eventide.

The swanherds where their sedges are
　Moved on in sunset's golden breath,
The shepherde lads I heard afarre,
　And my sonne's wife, Elizabeth;
Till floating o'er the grassy sea
Came downe that kyndly message free,
The "Brides of Mavis Enderby."

Then some looked uppe into the sky,
　And all along where Lindis flows
To where the goodly vessels lie,
　And where the lordly steeple shows.
They sayde, "And why should this thing be?
What danger lowers by land or sea?
They ring the tune of Enderby!

"For evil news from Mablethorpe,
　Of pyrate galleys warping down;
For shippes ashore beyond the scorpe,
　They have not spared to wake the towne:
But while the west bin red to see,
And storms be none, and pyrates flee,
Why ring 'The Brides of Enderby'?"

I looked without, and lo! my sonne
　Came riding downe with might and main:

He raised a shout as he drew on,
   Till all the welkin rang again,
"Elizabeth! Elizabeth!"
   (A sweeter woman ne'er drew breath
   Than my sonne's wife, Elizabeth.)

"The olde sea wall (he cried) is downe,
   The rising tide comes on apace,
And boats adrift in yonder towne
   Go sailing uppe the market-place."
He shook as one that looks on death:
"God save you, mother!" straight he saith;
"Where is my wife, Elizabeth?"

"Good sonne, where Lindis winds away,
   With her two bairns I marked her long;
And ere yon bells beganne to play
   Afar I heard her milking song."
He looked across the grassy lea,
To right, to left, "Ho Enderby!"
They rang "The Brides of Enderby!"

With that he cried and beat his breast;
   For, lo! along the river's bed
A mighty eygre reared his crest,
   And uppe the Lindis raging sped.
It swept with thunderous noises loud;
Shaped like a curling snow-white cloud,
Or like a demon in a shroud.

And rearing Lindis backward pressed
   Shook all her trembling bankes amaine;
Then madly at the eygre's breast
   Flung uppe her weltering walls again.
Then bankes came downe with ruin and rout—
Then beaten foam flew round about—
Then all the mighty floods were out.

So farre, so fast the eygre drave,
  The heart had hardly time to beat,
Before a shallow seething wave
  Sobbed in the grasses at oure feet:
The feet had hardly time to flee
Before it brake against the knee,
And all the world was in the sea.

Upon the roofe we sate that night;
  The noise of bells went sweeping by.
I marked the lofty beacon light
  Stream from the church-tower, red and high—
A lurid mark and dread to see;
And awsome bells they were to mee,
That in the dark rang "Enderby."

They rang the sailor lads to guide
  From roofe to roofe who fearless rowed,
And I—my sonne was at my side,
  And yet the ruddy beacon glowed;
And yet he moaned beneath his breath,
"O come in life, or come in death!
O lost! my love, Elizabeth."

And didst thou visit him no more?
  Thou didst, thou didst, my daughter deare;
The waters laid thee at his doore,
  Ere yet the early dawn was clear.
Thy pretty bairns in fast embrace,
The lifted sun shone on thy face,
Downe drifted to thy dwelling-place.

That flow strewed wrecks about the grass,
  That ebbe swept out the flocks to sea;
A fatal ebbe and flow, alas!
  To manye more than myne and mee:
But each will mourn his own (she saith),

And sweeter woman ne'er drew breath
Than my sonne's wife, Elizabeth.

I shall never hear her more
By the reedy Lindis shore,
"Cusha! Cusha! Cusha!" calling,
Ere the early dews be falling;
I shall never hear her song,
"Cusha! Cusha!" all along
Where the sunny Lindis floweth,
    Goeth, floweth;
From the meads where melick groweth,
When the water winding down,
Onward floweth to the town.

I shall never see her more
Where the reeds and rushes quiver,
    Shiver, quiver;
Stand beside the sobbing river,
Sobbing, throbbing, in its falling
To the sandy lonesome shore;
I shall never hear her calling,
Leave your meadow grasses mellow,
    Mellow, mellow;
Quit your cowslips, cowslips yellow;
Come uppe Whitefoot, come uppe Lightfoot;
Quit your pipes of parsley hollow,
    Hollow, hollow;
Come uppe Lightfoot, rise and follow;
    Lightfoot, Whitefoot,
From your clovers lift the head;
Come uppe Jetty, follow, follow,
Jetty, to the milking shed.

                J. Ingelow.

THE SANDS OF DEE.

"OH, Mary, go and call the cattle home,
   And call the cattle home,
   And call the cattle home,
  Across the sands of Dee."
The western wind was wild and dark with foam,
  And all alone went she.

  The western tide crept up along the sand,
   And o'er and o'er the sand,
   And round and round the sand,
  As far as eye could see.
The rolling mist came down and hid the land:
  And never home came she.

"Oh! is it weed, or fish, or floating hair—
   A tress of golden hair,
   A drownéd maiden's hair,
  Above the nets at sea?"
Was never salmon yet that shone so fair
  Among the stakes of Dee!

  They rowed her in across the rolling foam,
   The cruel crawling foam,
   The cruel hungry foam,
  To her grave beside the sea.
But still the boatmen hear her call the cattle home,
  Across the sands of Dee.

Charles Kingsley.

THREE FISHERS.

THREE fishers went sailing out into the west,
  Out into the west, as the sun went down;
Each thought of the woman who loved him best,
  And the children stood watching them out of the town.
For men must work, and women must weep,
And there's little to earn, and many to keep,
  Though the harbour-bar be moaning.

Three wives sat up in the lighthouse tower,
  And they trimmed the lamps as the sun went down;
They looked at the squall, and they looked at the shower,
  And the night-rack came rolling up ragged and brown;
But men must work, and women must weep,
Though storms be sudden, and waters deep,
  And the harbour-bar be moaning.

Three corpses lay out on the shining sands,
  In the morning gleam, as the tide went down;
And the women are weeping and wringing their hands,
  For those who will never come back to the town.
For men must work, and women must weep,
And the sooner it's over, the sooner to sleep,
  And good-bye to the bar and its moaning.

C. Kingsley.

THE STORM.

(MEG BLANE.)

"LORD, hearken to me!
   Save all poor souls at sea!
Thy breath is on their cheeks,—
   Their cheeks are wan wi' fear;
Nae man speaks,
   For wha could hear?
The wild white water screams,
   The wind cries loud;
The fireflaught gleams
   On tattered sail and shroud!
Under the red mast-light
   The hissing waters slip;
Thick reeks the storm o' night
   Round him that steers the ship,—
And his een are blind,
   And he knows not where they run.
LORD, be kind!
   Whistle back Thy wind,
For the sake of CHRIST Thy Son!"

... And as she prayed she knelt not on her knee,
But, standing on the threshold, looked to Sea,
   Where all was blackness and a watery roar,
Save when the dead light, flickering far away,
   Flash'd on the line of foam upon the shore,
And showed the ribs of reef and surging bay!
   There was no sign of life across the dark,
   No piteous light from fishing-boat or bark,
Albeit for such she hush'd her heart to pray.

With tattered plaid wrapt tight around her form,
  She stood a space, spat on by wind and rain,
Then, sighing deep, and turning from the Storm,
  She crept into her lonely hut again.

'Twas but a wooden hut under the height,
  Shielded in the black shadow of the crag:
One blow of such a wind as blew that night
  Could rend so rude a dwelling like a rag.
There, gathering in the crannies overhead,
Down fell the spouting rain heavy as lead,—
  So that the old roof and the rafters thin
Dript desolately, looking on the surf,
While blacker rain-drops down the walls of turf
  Splash'd momently on the mud-floor within.
There, swinging from the beam, an earthen lamp
Waved to the wind and glimmered in the damp,
  And shining in the chamber's wretchedness,
Illumed the household things of the poor place,
And flicker'd faintly on the woman's face,
  Sooted with rain, and on her dripping dress.
      A miserable den wherein to dwell,
      And yet she loved it well.

     "O Mither, are ye there?"
A deep voice filled the dark; she thrill'd to hear;
  With hard hand she pushed back her wild wet hair,
And kissed him. "Whisht, my bairn, for Mither's near."
  Then on the shuttle bed a figure thin
     Sat rubbing sleepy eyes:
  A bearded man, with heavy hanging chin,
    And on his face a light not over-wise.
"Water!" he said; and deep his thirst was quelled
Out of the broken pitcher she upheld,

And yawning sleepily, he gazed around,
And stretch'd his limbs again, and soon slept sound.
Stooping, she smooth'd his pillow 'neath his head,
　Still looking down with eyes liquid and mild,
And while she gazed, softly he slumberëd,
　　That bearded man, her child.
　And a child's dreams were his; for as he lay,
　He uttered happy cries as if at play,
　And his strong hand was lifted up on high
　As if to catch the bird or butterfly;
And often to his bearded lips there came
　　That lonely woman's name;
And though the wrath of Ocean roared so near,
　　That one sweet word
　　Was all the woman heard,
　And all she cared to hear.

　　Who did not know Meg Blane?
What hearth but heard the deeds that Meg had done?
　　What fisher of the main
But knew her, and her little-witted son?
For in the wildest waves of that wild coast
Her black boat hover'd and her net was tost,
And lonely in the watery solitude
The son and mother fished for daily food.
When on calm nights the herring hosts went by,
　Her frail boat followed the red smacks from shore,
And steering in the stern the man would lie
　While Meg was hoisting sail or plying oar;
Till, a black speck against the morning sky,
　The boat came homeward, with its silver store.
And Meg was cunning in the ways of things,
　Watching what every changing lineament
　Of Wind and Sky and Cloud and Water meant,
Knowing how Nature threatens ere she springs.

She knew the clouds as shepherds know their sheep,
  To eyes unskilled alike, yet different each;
She knew the wondrous voices of the Deep;
  The tones of sea-birds were to her a speech.

*   ÷   *   *

It was a night of summer, yet the wind
  Had wafted from God's wastes the rain-clouds dank,
Blown out Heaven's thousand eyes and left it blind,
  Though now and then the Moon gleamed moist behind
    The rack, till, smitten by the drift, she sank.
      But the Deep roared;
Sucked to the black clouds, spumed the foam-fleck'd main,
  While Lightning rent the storm-rack like a sword,
And earthward rolled the gray smoke of the Rain.

'Tis late, and yet the woman doth not rest,
But sitteth with chin drooping on her breast:
Weary she is, yet will not take repose;
Tired are her eyes, and yet they cannot close;
She rocketh to and fro upon her chair,
    And stareth at the air!

Far, far away her thoughts were travelling:
  They could not rest—they wandered far and fleet,
As the storm-petrels o'er the waters wing,
  And cannot find a place to rest their feet;
And in her ear a thin voice murmurëd,
    "If he be *dead*—be *dead!*"
Then, even then, the woman's face went white
  And awful, and her eyes were fixed in fear,
For suddenly all the wild screams of night
  Were hushed: the Wind lay down; and she could hear
Strange voices gather round her in the gloom,
Sounds of invisible feet across the room,

And after that the rustle of a shroud,
    And then a creaking door,
And last the coronach, full shrill and loud,
Of women clapping hands and weeping sore.

Now Meg knew well that ill was close at hand,
    On water or on land,
Because the Glamour touched her lids like breath,
  And scorch'd her heart: but in a waking swoon,
Quiet she stayed,— not stirring,—cold as death,
    And felt those voices croon;
Then suddenly she heard a human shout,
The hurried falling of a foot without,
Then a hoarse voice—a knocking at the door—
  "Meg, Meg! A Ship ashore!"

Now mark the woman! She hath risen her height,
Her dripping plaid is wrapt around her tight;
Tight clenchëd in her palm her fingers are;
Her eye is steadfast as a fixëd star.
One look upon her child—he sleepeth on—
One step unto the door, and she is gone:
Barefooted out into the dark she fares,
  And comes where, rubbing eyelids thick with sleep,
The half-clad fishers mingle oaths and prayers,
    And look upon the Deep.

    . . . Black was the oozy lift,
    Black were the sea and land;
Hither and thither, thick with foam and drift,
    Did the deep Waters shift,
  Swinging with iron clash on stone and sand.
Faintlier the heavy Rain was falling,
Faintlier, faintlier the Wind was calling

With hollower echoes up the drifting dark!
While the swift rockets shooting through the night
Flash'd past the foam-flecked reef with phantom light,
    And showed the piteous outline of the bark,
Rising and falling like a living thing,
        Shuddering, shivering,
While, howling beastlike, the white breakers there
Spat blindness in the dank eyes of despair.
Then one cried, "She has sunk!"—and on the shore
    Men shook, and on the heights the women cried;
But, lo! the outline of the bark once more!
    While flashing faint the blue light rose and died.
Ah, GOD, put out Thy hand! all for the sake
Of little ones, and weary hearts that wake!
    Be gentle! chain the fierce waves with a chain!
Let the gaunt seaman's little boys and girls
Sit on his knee and play with his black curls
        Yet once again!
And breathe the frail lad safely through the foam
Back to the hungry mother in her home!
And spare the bad man with the frenzied eye;
Kiss *him*, for CHRIST'S sake, bid Thy Death go by—
        He hath no heart to die!

Now faintlier blew the wind, the thin rain ceased,
    The thick cloud cleared like smoke from off the strand
For, lo! a bright blue glimmer in the East,—
        GOD putting out His hand!
And overhead the rack grew thinner too,
        And through the smoky gorge
The Wind drave past the stars, and faint they flew
        Like sparks blown from a forge!
And now the thousand foam-flames o' the Sea
        Hither and thither flashing visibly;
And gray lights hither and thither came and fled,
Like dim shapes searching for the drownĕd dead;

And where these shapes most thickly glimmer'd by,
  Out on the cruel reef the black hulk lay,
And cast, against the kindling eastern sky,
  Its shape gigantic on the shrouding spray.

Silent upon the shore, the fishers fed
    Their eyes on horror, waiting for the close,
    When in the midst of them a shrill voice rose:
      "The boat! the boat!" it said.
Like creatures startled from a trance, they turned
    To her who spake; tall in the midst stood she,
With arms uplifted, and with eyes that yearned
        Out on the murmuring Sea.
Some, shrugging shoulders, homeward turned their eyes,
    And others answered back in brutal speech;
But some, strong-hearted, uttering shouts and cries,
    Followed the fearless woman up the beach.
A rush to seaward—black confusion—then
    A struggle with the surf upon the strand—
'Mid shrieks of women, cries of desperate men,
    The long oars smite, the black boat springs from land!
        Around the thick spray flies;
The waves roll on and seem to overwhelm.
    With blowing hair and onward-gazing eyes
The woman stands erect, and grips the helm. . . .

Now fearless heart, Meg Blane, or all must die!
Let not the skill'd hand thwart the steadfast eye!
The crested wave comes near,—crag-like it towers
Above you, scattering round its chilly showers:
One flutter of the hand, and all is done!
Now steel thy heart, thou woman-hearted one!
        Softly the good helm guides;
Round to the liquid ridge the boat leaps light,—
Hidden an instant,—on the foamy height,
    Dripping and quivering like a bird, it rides.

Athwart the ragged rift the Moon looms pale,
  Driven before the gale,
And making silvern shadows with her breath,
Where on the sighing Sea it shimmereth;
And, lo! the light illumes the reef; 'tis shed
  Full on the wreck, as the dark boat draws nigh.
A crash!—the wreck upon the reef is fled!
  A scream!—and all is still beneath the sky,
  Save the wild waters as they whirl and cry.

Robert Buchanan.

LONGING FOR HOME.

1.

A song of a boat:—
There was once a boat on a billow:
Lightly she rocked to her port remote,
And the foam was white in her wake like snow,
And her frail mast bowed when the breeze would blow,
  And bent like a wand of willow.

2.

I shaded mine eyes one day when a boat
  Went curtseying over the billow;
I marked her course till a dancing mote
She faded out on the moonlit foam,
And I stayed behind in the dear loved home;
  And my thoughts all day were about the boat
  And my dreams upon the pillow.

3.

I pray you hear my song of a boat,
  For it is but short:—
My boat, you shall find none fairer afloat,
  In river or port.

Long I looked out for the lad she bore,
    On the open desolate sea,
And I think he sailed to the heavenly shore,
    For he came not back to me—
                Ah me!

4.

A song of a nest:—
There was once a nest in a hollow:
Down in the mosses and knot-grass pressed,
    Soft and warm, and full to the brim—
Vetches leaned over it purple and dim,
    With buttercup buds to follow.

5.

I pray you hear my song of a nest,
    For it is not long:—
You shall never light, in a summer quest
    The bushes among—
Shall never light on a prouder sitter,
    A fairer nestful, nor ever know
A softer sound than their tender twitter,
    That wind-like did come and go.

6.

I had a nestful once of my own,
    Ah happy, happy I!
Right dearly I loved them: but when they were grown
    They spread out their wings to fly—
O, one after one they flew away
    Far up to the heavenly blue,
To the better country, the upper day,
    And—I wish I was going too.

7.

I pray you, what is the nest to me,
    My empty nest?
And what is the shore where I stood to see
    My boat sail down to the west?

Can I call that home where I anchor yet,
   Though my good man has sailed?
Can I call that home where my nest was set,
   Now all its hope hath failed?
Nay, but the port where my sailor went,
   And the land where my nestlings be:
There is the home where my thoughts are sent,
   The only home for me—
          Ah me!

                 J. Ingelow.

DEATH.

THEY die—the dead return not. Misery
  Sits near an open grave, and calls them over,
A youth with hoary hair and haggard eye.
  They are the names of kindred, friend, and lover,
Which he so feebly calls. They all are gone,
Fond wretch, all dead! Those vacant names alone,
    This most familiar scene, my pain,
     These tombs,—alone remain.

Misery, my sweetest friend, oh! weep no more!
  Thou wilt not be consoled? I wonder not:
For I have seen thee from thy dwelling's door
  Watch the calm sunset with them, and this spot
  Was even as bright and calm but transitory,—
  And now thy hopes are gone, thy hair is hoary.
    This most familiar scene, my pain,
     These tombs,—alone remain.

              P. B. Shelley.

AIRLY BEACON.

AIRLY Beacon, Airly Beacon;
  Oh, the pleasant sight to see
Shires and towns from Airly Beacon,
  While my love climbed up to me!

Airly Beacon, Airly Beacon,
  Oh, the happy hours we lay
Deep in fern on Airly Beacon,
  Courting through the summer's day!

Airly Beacon, Airly Beacon;
  Oh, the weary haunt for me
All alone on Airly Beacon,
  With his baby on my knee!

C. Kingsley.

THE MERRY LARK WAS UP AND SINGING.

THE merry, merry lark was up and singing,
  And the hare was out and feeding on the lea;
And the merry merry bells below were ringing,
  When my child's laugh rang through me.

Now the hare is snared and dead beside the snow-yard
  And the lark beside the dreary winter sea;
And the baby in his cradle in the churchyard
  Sleeps sound till the bell brings me.

C. Kingsley

LAMENT.

Break, break, break,
  On thy cold gray stones, O Sea!
And I would that my tongue could utter
  The thoughts that arise in me.

O well for the fisherman's boy,
  That he shouts with his sister at play!
O well for the sailor lad,
  That he sings in his boat on the bay!

And the stately ships go on
  To their haven under the hill;
But O for the touch of a vanish'd hand,
  And the sound of a voice that is still!

Break, break, break,
  At the foot of thy crags, O Sea!
But the tender grace of a day that is dead
  Will never come back to me.

A. Tennyson.

A LAMENT.

I STAND where I last stood with thee!
    Sorrow, Oh sorrow!
There is not a leaf on the trysting tree;
There is not a joy on the earth for me;
    Sorrow, Oh sorrow!
When shalt thou be once again what thou wert?
Oh the sweet yesterdays fled from the heart!
    Have they a morrow?
Here we stood, ere we parted, so close side by side;
Two lives that once part are as ships that divide
When, moment on moment there rushes between
    The one and the other, a sea;—
Ah, never can fall from the days that have been
    A gleam on the years that shall be!

E. Bulwer, Lord Lytton.

ALONE.

FROM the close-shut windows gleams no spark;
The night is chilly, the night is dark,
The poplars shiver, the pine-trees moan,
My hair by the autumn breeze is blown,
Under thy window I sing alone,
Alone, alone, ah woe! alone!

The darkness is pressing coldly around,
The windows shake with a lonely sound,
The stars are hid and the night is drear,
The heart of silence throbs in mine ear,
In thy chamber thou sittest alone,
Alone, alone, ah woe! alone!

The world is happy, the world is wide,
Kind hearts are beating on every side;
Ah, why should we lie so coldly curled
Alone in the shell of this great world?
Why should we any more be alone?
Alone, alone, ah woe! alone!

O, 'tis a bitter and dreary word,
The saddest by man's ear ever heard!
We each are young, we each have a heart,
Why stand we ever coldly apart?
Must we for ever, then, be alone?
Alone, alone, ah woe! alone!

J. R. Lowell.

THE LOST HORIZON.

I STOOD at evening in the crimson air:
  The trees shook off their dusky twilight glow;
The wind took up old burdens of despair,
  And moaned like Atlas with his world of woe.

Like the great circle of a bronzèd ring
  That clasped the vision of the vanished day,
I saw the vague horizon vanishing
  Around me into darkness, far away.

Then, while the night came fast with cloudy roar,
  Lo, all around me rays of hearths unknown
Sprang from the gloom with light unseen before,
  And made a warm horizon of their own.

I sighed: "The wanderer in the desert sees
  Strange ghosts of summer lands arising, sweet
With restless waters, green with gracious trees
  Whose shadows beckon welcome to his feet.

"For erst, where now the desert far away
  Stretches a wilderness of hopeless sand,
Clasping fair fields and sunburnt harvests lay
  The heavenly girdles of a fruitful land."

I thought of a sweet mirage now no more:
  Warm windows radiant with a dancing flame—
Dear voices heard within a happy door—
  A face that to the darkness, lighted, came.

No hearth of mine was waiting, near or far;
  No threshold for my coming footstep yearned
To touch its slumber; no warm window-star,
  The tender Venus, to my longing burned.

The darkened windows slowly lost their fire,
  But shimmered with the ghostly ember-light:
A wanderer, with old embers of desire,
  The lost horizon held me in the night
                              John James Piatt.

ASSOCIATIONS.

YOU know the place is just the same!
  The rooks build here: the sandy hill is
Ablaze with broom, as when she came
Across the sea with her new name,
  To dwell among the moated lilies.

The trifoly is on the walls:
  The daisies in the bowling alley:
The ox at eve lows from the stalls:
At eve the cuckoo, floating, calls,
  When foxgloves tremble in the valley.

The iris blows from court to court:
  The bald white spider flits, or stays in
The chinks behind the dragonwort;
That Triton still, at his old sport,
  Blows bubbles in his broken basin.

The terrace where she used to walk
  Still shines at noon between the roses:
The garden-paths are blind with chalk:
The dragonfly from stalk to stalk
  Swims sparkling blue till evening closes.

Then, just above that long dark copse,
 One warm red star comes out, and passes
Westward, and mounts, and mounts, and stops
(Or seems to) o'er the turret-tops,
 And lights those lonely casement-glasses.

Sir Ralph still wears that old grim smile.
 The staircase creaks as up I clamber
To those still rooms, to muse awhile.
I see the little meadow-stile
 As I lean from the great south-chamber.

And Lady Ruth is just as white.
 (Ah, still the face seems strangely like her!)
The lady and the wicked knight—
All just the same—she swoon'd for fright—
 And he—his arm still raised to strike her.

Her boudoir—no one enters there:
 The very flowers which last she gather'd
Are in the vase; the lute—the chair—
And all things—just as then they were!
 Except the jasmines—those are wither'd.

But when along the corridors
 The last red pause of day is streaming,
I seem to hear her up the floors:
I seem to see her thro' the doors:
 And then I know that I am dreaming.

      Owen Meredith (Lord Lytton

LEAVING THE OLD HOME.

UNWATCH'D, the garden bough shall sway,
  The tender blossom flutter down;
  Unlov'd that beech will gather brown,
This maple burn itself away;

Unloved, the sun-flower, shining fair,
  Ray round with flames her disc of seed,
  And many a rose-carnation feed
With summer spice the humming air;

Unloved, by many a sandy bar,
  The brook shall babble down the plain,
  At noon or when the lesser wain
Is twisting round the polar star;

Uncared for, gird the windy grove
  And flood the haunts of hern and crake;
  Or into silver arrows break
The sailing moon in creek and cove;

Till from the garden and the wild
  A fresh association blow,
  And year by year the landscape grow
Familiar to the stranger's child;

As year by year the labourer tills
  His wonted glebe, or lops the glades;
  And year by year our memory fades
From all the circle of the hills.

A. Tennyson.

I REMEMBER, I REMEMBER.

I REMEMBER, I remember,
The house where I was born,
The little window where the sun
Came peeping in at morn;
He never came a wink too soon,
Nor brought too long a day,
But now, I often wish the night
Had borne my breath away!

I remember, I remember,
The roses, red and white,
The violets, and the lily-cups,
Those flowers made of light!
The lilacs where the robin built,
And where my brother set
The laburnum on his birth-day,—
The tree is living yet!

I remember, I remember,
Where I was used to swing,
And thought the air must rush as fresh
To swallows on the wing;
My spirit flew in feathers then,
That is so heavy now,
And summer pools could hardly cool
The fever on my brow!

I remember, I remember,
The fir trees dark and high;
I used to think their slender tops
Were close against the sky:
It was a childish ignorance,
But now 'tis little joy
To know I'm farther off from Heav'n
Than when I was a boy.

T. Hood.

THE LIGHT OF OTHER DAYS.

OFT in the stilly night
  Ere slumber's chain has bound me,
Fond Memory brings the light
  Of other days around me;
    The smiles, the tears
    Of boyhood's years,
  The words of love then spoken
    The eyes that shone,
    Now dimm'd and gone,
  The cheerful hearts now broken!
Thus in the stilly night
  Ere slumber's chain has bound me,
Sad Memory brings the light
  Of other days around me.

When I remember all
  The friends so link'd together
I've seen around me fall
  Like leaves in wintry weather,
    I feel like one
    Who treads alone
  Some banquet-hall deserted,
    Whose lights are fled,
    Whose garlands dead,
  And all but he departed!

17*

Thus in the stilly night
  Ere slumber's chain has bound me,
Sad Memory brings the light
  Of other days around me.

T. Moore.

THE RECOLLECTION.

Now the last day of many days
All beautiful and bright as thou,
The loveliest and the last, is dead,
Rise, Memory, and write its praise!
Up, do thy wonted work! come, trace
The epitaph of glory fled,
For now the Earth has changed its face.
A frown is on the Heaven's brow.

We wander'd to the Pine Forest
  That skirts the Ocean's foam;
The lightest wind was in its nest,
  The tempest in its home.
The whispering waves were half asleep,
  The clouds were gone to play,
And on the bosom of the deep
  The smile of Heaven lay;
It seem'd as if the hour were one
  Sent from beyond the skies
Which scatter'd from above the sun
  A light of Paradise!

We paused amid the pines that stood
  The giants of the waste,
Tortured by storms to shapes as rude
  As serpents interlaced,—

And soothed by every azure breath
   That under heaven is blown
To harmonies and hues beneath,
   As tender as its own:
Now all the tree-tops lay asleep
   Like green waves on the sea,
As still as in the silent deep
   The ocean-woods may be.

How calm it was!—the silence there
   By such a chain was bound,
That even the busy woodpecker
   Made stiller by her sound
The inviolable quietness;
   The breath of peace we drew
With its soft motion made not less
   The calm that round us grew.
There seem'd from the remotest seat
   Of the wide mountain waste
To the soft flower beneath our feet
   A magic circle traced,
A spirit interfused around,
   A thrilling silent life;
To momentary peace it bound
   Our mortal nature's strife;—
And still I felt the centre of
   The magic circle there
Was one fair Form that fill'd with love
   The lifeless atmosphere.

We paused beside the pools that lie
   Under the forest bough;
Each seem'd as 'twere a little sky
   Gulf'd in a world below;

A firmament of purple light
    Which in the dark earth lay,
More boundless than the depth of night
    And purer than the day—
In which the lovely forests grew
    As in the upper air,
More perfect both in shape and hue
    Than any spreading there.
There lay the glade and neighbouring lawn,
    And through the dark green wood
The white sun twinkling like the dawn
    Out of a speckled cloud.
Sweet views which in our world above
    Can never well be seen
Were imaged by the water's love
    Of that fair forest green:
And all was interfused beneath
    With an Elysian glow,
An atmosphere without a breath,
    A softer day below.
Like one beloved, the scene had lent
    To the dark water's breast
Its every leaf and lineament
    With more than truth exprest;
Until an envious wind crept by,
    Like an unwelcome thought
Which from the mind's too faithful eye
    Blots one dear image out.
—Though Thou art ever fair and kind,
    The forests ever green,
Less oft is peace in Shelley's mind
    Than calm in waters seen!

P. B. Shelley.

LOVE HOUSELESS.

1.

THE cold earth slept below;
Above, the cold sky shone;
   And all around,
   With a chilling sound,
From caves of ice and fields of snow
The breath of night like death did flow
   Beneath the sinking moon.

2.

The wintry hedge was black;
The green grass was not seen;
   The birds did rest
   On the bare thorn's breast,
Whose roots, beside the pathway track,
Had bound their folds o'er many a crack
   Which the frost had made between.

3.

Thine eyes glowed in the glare
Of the moon's dying light.
   As a fen-fire's beam
   On a sluggish stream
Gleams dimly, so the moon shone there;
And it yellowed the strings of thy tangled hair,
   That shook in the wind of night.

4.

The moon made thy lips pale, beloved;
   The wind made thy bosom chill;
   The night did shed
   On thy dear head
Its frozen dew, and thou didst lie
Where the bitter breath of the naked sky
   Might visit thee at will.

P. B. Shelley.

A PARTING IN DREAMLAND.

Ἄδιστος ἀφεμένων.

AMONG the poppies by the well
    Of Lethe, where I weary lay,
Upon my soul a slumber fell,
    Making the light of summer grey;
Nepenthé too I ate of him,
Whose eyes were eyes of Seraphim.

But ere I slept, while still it seemed
    That sleep was a delicious thing,
The splendour of a vision streamed
    Above the poppy-heads that fling
Their drowsy juice and drowsy scent
Through blood and brain with ravishment.

For there He stood whose eyes are eyes
    Of Seraphim: and lo! his lips
Seemed quivering with the winds of sighs;
    And all his forehead in eclipse
Burned not, but showered well-heads of tears
Amid the deserts of dead years.

Yea, and his heart fed living fire;
    And both his cheeks like ashes wan
Were cinders of a spent desire
    For lack of food to feed upon:
Therewith the Spirit smiled and spake
Words sweet as breath from buds that break:

"I go; take now, dear soul, thy rest;
    Slumber beneath the poppy-flowers!
The mole within her winter nest
    Be not so folded from sad hours
As thou, who of the thought of me
Eatest Nepenthé wearily.

"I go; but when thy dream is o'er,
    When thou awakest cold perchance,
And haply from sleep's golden door
    Gazest upon the drear expanse
Of barren years and vacant life
And long monotony of strife,

"Think then of me: though hence I go;
    Though I am withered, worn, and old,
With waiting, praying, weeping through
    Long days that shiver in the cold
Of thy scant love—yet will I come,
And, when thou callest, bear thee home."

He spake; and fire with sudden pain
    Flashed in his face.   Then slumber fell
Upon my lids like summer rain;
    And through faint dreams the terrible
Flame of that head, of those wild eyes,
Died; and my sleep was Paradise.

John Addington Symonds.

LOVED ONCE.

I CLASSED, appraising once,
Earth's lamentable sounds; the "well-a-day,"
  The jarring "yea" and "nay,"
The fall of kisses on unanswering clay,
The sobbed "farewell," the "welcome" mournfuller;—
  But all did leaven the air
With a less bitter leaven of sure despair,
  Than these words—"I loved once."

And who saith, "I loved once?"
Not angels, whose clear eyes love, love foresee,
  Love through eternity!
Who, by to love, do apprehend to be.
Not God, called Love, his noble crown-name,— casting
  A light too broad for blasting!
The Great God, changing not from everlasting,
  Saith never, "I loved once."

Oh, never is "Loved once."
Thy word, thou Victim-Christ, misprized friend?
  Thy cross and curse may rend;
But, having loved, Thou lovest to the end!
It is man's saying—man's! Too weak to move
  One sphered star above,
Man desecrates the eternal God-word, love,
  With his "no more," and "once."

How say ye, "We loved once,"
Blasphemers? Is your earth not cold enow,
   Mourners, without that snow?
Ah, friends! and would ye wrong each other so?
And could ye say of some, whose love is known,
   Whose prayers have met your own,
Whose tears have fallen for you, whose smiles have
       shone,
   Such words, "We loved them once?"

   Could ye "We loved her once"
Say calm of me, sweet friends, when out of sight?
   When hearts of better right
Stand in between me and your happy light?
And when, as flowers kept too long in shade,
   Ye find my colours fade,
And all that is not love in me, decayed?
   Such words, "Ye loved me once!"

   Could ye "We loved her once"
Say cold of me, when further put away
   In earth's sepulchral clay?
When mute the lips which deprecate to day?—
Not so! not then—least then! When life is shriven,
   And death's full joy is given;
Of those who sit and love you up in heaven
   Say not, "We loved them once."

   Say never, ye loved once!
God is too near above, the grave beneath,
   And all our moments breathe
Too quick in mysteries of life and death,
For such a word. The eternities avenge
   Affections light of range—
There comes no change to justify that change,
   Whatever comes—loved once!

And yet that same word "once"
Is humanly acceptive! Kings have said,
  Shaking a discrowned head,
"We ruled once;"—dotards, "We once taught and led;"–
Cripples once danced i' the vines; and bards approved
  Were once by scornings moved;
But love strikes one hour—love. Those never loved
  Who dream that they loved once.

E. B. Browning.

VIVIEN'S SONG.

In love, if love be love, if love be ours,
Faith and unfaith can ne'er be equal powers:
Unfaith in aught is want of faith in all.

It is the little rift within the lute,
That by and by will make the music mute,
And ever widening slowly silence all.

The little rift within the lover's lute,
Or little pitted speck in garnered fruit,
That rotting inward slowly moulders all.

It is not worth the keeping; let it go:
But shall it? answer, darling, answer, no.
And trust me not at all, or all in all.

A. Tennyson.

ELAINE'S SONG.

"SWEET is true love tho' given in vain, in vain;
And sweet is Death who puts an end to pain:
I know not which is sweeter—no, not I.

"Love, art thou sweet? then bitter Death must be:
Love, thou art bitter: sweet is Death to me.
O Love, if death be sweeter, let me die.

"Sweet Love, that seems not made to fade away,
Sweet Death, that seems to make us loveless clay,
I know not which is sweeter—no, not I.

"I fain would follow Love, if that could be;
I needs must follow Death, who calls for me;
Call and I follow, I follow! Let me die."

A. Tennyson.

LOVE AND DEATH.

WHAT time the mighty moon was gathering light,
Love paced the thymy plots of Paradise,
And all about him rolled his lustrous eyes;
When, turning round a cassia, full in view,.
Death, walking all alone beneath a yew,
And talking to himself, first met his sight:
"You must begone," said Death, "these walks are mine."
Love wept and spread his sheeny vans for flight;
Yet, ere he parted, said,—"This hour is thine;
Thou art the shadow of life; and as the tree
Stands in the sun and shadows all beneath,
So in the light of great eternity
Life eminent creates the shade of death;
The shadow passeth when the tree shall fall,
But I shall reign for ever over all."

A. Tennyson.

LOVE—A SONNET.

I THOUGHT once how Theocritus had sung
Of the sweet years, the dear and wished-for years,
Who each one, in a gracious hand, appears
To bear a gift for mortals, old and young;
And as I mused it in his antique tongue,
I saw a gradual vision through my tears,
The sweet sad years, the melancholy years,
Those of my own life, who by turns had flung
A shadow across me.   Straightway I was 'ware.
So weeping, how a mystic shape did move
Behind me, and drew me backwards by the hair,
And a voice said in mastery, while I strove,
"Guess now who holds thee?" "Death," I said; but there
  The silver answer rang, — "Not Death, but Love."

E. B. Browning.

LOVESIGHT.

WHEN do I see thee most, beloved one?
  When in the light the spirits of mine eyes
  Before thy face, their altar, solemnize
The worship of that Love through thee made known!
Or when in the dusk hours, (we two alone,)
  Close-kissed and eloquent of still replies
  Thy twilight-hidden glimmering visage lies,
And my soul only sees thy soul its own?
O love, my love! if I no more should see
Thyself, nor on the earth the shadow of thee,
  Nor image of thine eyes in any spring,—
How then should sound upon Life's darkening slope
The ground-whirl of the perished leaves of Hope,
  The wind of Death's imperishable wing?

Dante Gabriel Rossetti.

EVENING.

ALREADY evening! In the duskiest nook
   Of yon dusk corner, under the Death's-head,
   Between the alembics, thrust this legended
And iron-bound, and melancholy book;
For I will read no longer. The loud brook
   Shelves his sharp light up shallow banks thin-spread;
   The slumbrous west grows slowly red, and red:
Up from the ripen'd corn her silver hook
   The moon is lifting: and deliciously
Along the warm blue hills the day declines.
   The first star brightens while she waits for me,
   And round her swelling heart the zone grows tight:
Musing, half-sad, in her soft hair she twines
   The white rose, whispering "He will come to-night!"

Owen Meredith (Lord Lytton).

AUTUMN.

THOU comest, Autumn, heralded by the rain,
With banners, by great gales incessant fanned,
Brighter than brightest silks of Samarcand,
And stately oxen harnessed to thy wain!
Thou standest, like imperial Charlemagne,
Upon thy bridge of gold; thy royal hand
Outstretched with benedictions o'er the land,
Blessing the farms through all thy vast domain.
Thy shield is the red harvest moon, suspended
So long beneath the heaven's o'erhanging eaves;
Thy steps are by the farmer's prayers attended;
Like flames upon an altar shine the sheaves;
And, following thee in thy ovation splendid,
Thine almoner, the wind, scatters the golden leaves.

H. W. Longfellow.

OCTOBER.

THE passionate summer's dead! The sky's aglow
  With roseate flushes of matur'd desire;
  The winds at eve are musical and low
  As sweeping chords of a lamenting lyre,
Far up among the pillared clouds of fire
  Whose pomp of strange procession upwards rolls
  With gorgeous blazonry of pictured scrolls,
  To celebrate the summer's past renown.
Ah me! How regally the heavens look down,
  O'ershadowing beautiful autumnal woods,
  And harvest-fields with hoarded increase brown,
And deep-toned majesty of golden floods
  That lift their solemn dirges to the sky,
  To swell the purple pomp that floateth by.

Paul H. Hayne.

THE INDIAN SUMMER.

IT is the season when the light of dreams
Around the year in golden glory lies;—
The heavens are full of floating mysteries,
And down the lake the veiléd splendour beams.
Like hidden poets lie the hazy streams,
Mantled with mysteries of their own romance,
While scarce a breath disturbs their drowsy trance.
The yellow leaf which down the soft air gleams,
Glides, wavers, falls, and skims the unruffled lake.
Here the frail maples and the faithful firs
By twisted vines are wed; the russet brake
Skirts the low pool; and starred with open burrs
The chesnut stands. But when the north-wind stirs,
How like an arméd host the summoned scene shall wake

Thomas Buchanan Read.

AUTUMN IDLENESS.

THIS sunlight shames November where he grieves
  In dead red leaves, and will not let him shun
  The day, though bough with bough be over-run;
But with a blessing every glade receives
High salutation; while from hillock-eaves
  The deer gaze calling, dappled white and dun,
  As if, being foresters of old, the sun
Had marked them with the shade of forest-leaves.
Here dawn to-day unveil'd her magic glass;
  Here noon now gives the thirst and takes the dew;
Till eve bring rest when other good things pass.
  And here the lost hours the lost hours renew
While I still lead my shadow o'er the grass,
Nor know, for longing, that which I should do.

                                    D. G. Rossetti.

IN SAN LORENZO.

Is thine hour come to wake, O slumbering Night?
  Hath not the Dawn a message in thine ear?
  Though thou be stone and sleep, yet shalt thou hear
When the word falls from heaven—Let there be Light.
Thou knowest we would not do thee the despite
  To wake thee while the old sorrow and shame were near;
  We spake not loud for thy sake, and for fear
Lest thou should'st lose the rest that was thy right,
The blessing given thee that was thine alone,
The happiness to sleep and to be stone.
  Yea, we kept silence of thee for thy sake,
Albeit we knew thee alive, and left with thee
The great good gift to feel not nor to see;
  But will not yet thine Angel bid thee wake?

A. C. Swinburne.

ON THE EXTINCTION
OF THE VENETIAN REPUBLIC.

ONCE did she hold the gorgeous East in fee,
And was the safeguard of the West: the worth
Of Venice did not fall below her birth—
Venice, the eldest child of Liberty!
She was a maiden city, bright and free;
No guile seduced, no force could violate;
And, when she took unto herself a mate,
She must espouse the everlasting sea.
And what if she had seen those glories fade,
Those titles vanish, and that strength decay;
Yet shall some tribute of regret be paid
When her long life hath reached its final day:
Men are we, and must grieve when even the shade
Of that which once was great is passed away.

W. Wordsworth.

FOR TITIAN.

THUS in a room he stood wherein there was
A marble bath, whose brimming water yet
Was scarcely still; a vessel of green glass
Half full of odorous ointment was there set
Upon the topmost step that still was wet,
And jewelled shoes and women's dainty gear,
Lay cast upon the varied pavement near.

In one quick glance these things his eyes did see,
But speedily they turned round to behold
Another sight, for throned on ivory
There sat a girl, whose dripping tresses rolled
On to the floor in waves of gleaming gold,
Cast back from such a form as, erewhile shown
To one poor shepherd, lighted up Troy town.

Naked she was, the kisses of her feet
Upon the floor a dying path had made
From the full bath unto her ivory seat;
In her right hand, upon her bosom laid,
She held a golden comb, a mirror weighed
Her left hand down, aback her fair head lay
Dreaming awake of some long-vanished day.

Her eyes were shut, but she seemed not to sleep,
Her lips were murmuring things unheard and low,
Or sometimes twitched as though she needs must weep
Though from her eyes the tears refused to flow;
And oft with heavenly red her cheek did glow,
As if remembrance of some half-sweet shame
Across the web of many memories came.

William Morris.

SONG.

My goblet's golden lips are dry,
   And, as the rose doth pine
   For dew, so doth for wine
     My goblet's cup;
Rain, O! rain, or it will die;
     Rain, fill it up!

Arise, and get thee wings to-night,
   Ætna! and let run o'er
   Thy wines, a hill no more,
     But darkly frown
A cloud, where eagles dare not soar,
     Dropping rain down!

T. L. Beddoes.

THE PHANTOM-WOOER.

A GHOST that loved a lady fair
Ever in the starry air
  Of midnight at her pillow stood;
And with a sweetness skies above
The luring words of human love
  Her soul the phantom wooed.
    Sweet and sweet is their poison'd note,
    The little snakes of silver throat
    In mossy skulls that nest and lie,
    Ever singing "Die, oh! die."

Young soul, put off your flesh, and come
With me into the silent tomb!
  Our bed is lovely, dark, and sweet;
The earth will swing us, as she goes,
Beneath our coverlid of snows,
  And the warm leaden sheet.
    Dear and dear is their poison'd note,
    The little snakes of silver throat
    In mossy skulls that nest and lie,
    Ever singing "Die, oh! die."

                              T. L. Beddoes.

THE CARD-DEALER.

COULD you not drink her gaze like wine?
  Yet though its splendour swoon
Into the silence languidly
  As a tune into a tune,
Those eyes unravel the coiled night
  And know the stars at noon.

The gold that's heaped beside her hand,
  In truth rich prize it were;
And rich the dreams that wreathe her brows
  With magic stillness there;
And he were rich that should unwind
  That woven golden hair.

Around her, where she sits, the dance
  Now breathes its eager heat;
And not more lightly or more true
  Fall there the dancer's feet
Than fall her cards on the bright board
  As 'twere an heart that beat.

Her fingers let them softly through,
  Smooth polished silent things;
And each one as it falls reflects
  In swift light-shadowings,
Blood-red and purple, green and blue,
  The great eyes of her rings.

Whom plays she with! With thee, who lov'st
   Those gems upon her hand;
With me, who search her secret brows;
   With all men, bless'd or bann'd.
We play together, she and we,
   Within a vain strange land:

A land without any order,—
   Day even as night, (one saith,)—
Where who lieth down ariseth not
   Nor the sleeper awakeneth;
A land of darkness as darkness itself,
   And of the shadow of death.

What be her cards, you ask! Even these:—
   The heart that doth but crave
More, having fed; the diamond
   Skilled to make base seem brave;
The club, for smiting in the dark;
   The spade, to dig a grave.

And do you ask what game she plays?
   With me 'tis lost or won;
With thee it is playing still; with him
   It is not well begun;
But 'tis a game she plays with all
   Beneath the sway o' the sun.

Thou seest the card that falls,—she knows
   The card that followeth:
Her game in thy tongue is called Life,
   As ebbs thy daily breath:
When she shall speak, thou'lt learn her tongue
   And know she calls it Death.

                              D. G. Rossetti.

YOUTH AND AGE

VERSE, a breeze 'mid blossoms straying,
Where Hope clung feeding, like a bee—
Both were mine! Life went a-maying
  With Nature, Hope, and Poesy,
    When I was young!
When I was young?—Ah, woful when!
Ah! for the change 'twixt Now and Then!
This breathing house not built with hands,
This body that does me grievous wrong,
O'er aery cliffs and glittering sands
How lightly then it flash'd along:
Like those trim skiffs, unknown of yore,
On winding lakes and rivers wide,
That ask no aid of sail or oar,
That fear no spite of wind or tide!
Nought cared this body for wind or weather
When Youth and I lived in't together.

Flowers are lovely; Love is flower-like;
Friendship is a sheltering tree;
O! the joys, that came down shower-like,
Of Friendship, Love, and Liberty,
    Ere I was old!

Ere I was old? Ah woful Ere,
Which tells me, Youth's no longer here!

O Youth! for years so many and sweet
'Tis known that Thou and I were one;
I'll think it but a fond conceit—
It cannot be, that Thou art gone!
Thy vesper-bell hath not yet toll'd:—
And thou wert aye a masker bold!
What strange disguise hast now put on
To make believe that thou art gone?
I see these locks in silvery slips,
This drooping gait, this alter'd size:
But Springtide blossoms on thy lips,
And tears take sunshine from thine eyes!
Life is but Thought: so think I will
That Youth and I are housemates still.

Dew-drops are the gems of morning,
But the tears of mournful eve!
Where no hope is, life's a warning
That only serves to make us grieve
　　　When we are old:
—That only serves to make us grieve
With oft and tedious taking-leave,
Like some poor nigh-related guest
That may not rudely be dismisst,
Yet hath out-stay'd his welcome while,
And tells the jest without the smile.

                              S. T. Coleridge.

GROWING OLD.

WHAT is it to grow old?
Is it to lose the glory of the form,
The lustre of the eye?
Is it for beauty to forego her wreath?
Yes, but not this alone.

Is it to feel our strength—
Not our bloom only, but our strength—decay?
Is it to feel each limb
Grow stiffer, every function less exact,
Each nerve more weakly strung?

Yes, this, and more! but not,
Ah, 'tis not what in youth we dream'd 'twould be!
'Tis not to have our life
Mellow'd and soften'd as with sunset glow,
A golden day's decline!

'Tis not to see the world
As from a height, with rapt prophetic eyes,
And heart profoundly stirr'd;
And weep, and feel the fulness of the past,
The years that are no more!

It is to spend long days
And not once feel that we were ever young.
It is to add, immured
In the hot prison of the present, month
To month with weary pain

It is to suffer this,
And feel but half, and feebly, what we feel.
Deep in our hidden heart
Festers the dull remembrance of a change,
But no emotion—none.

It is—last stage of all—
When we are frozen up within, and quite
The phantom of ourselves,
To hear the world applaud the hollow ghost
Which blamed the living man.

M. Arnold.

UP-HILL.

Does the road wind up-hill all the way?
   Yes, to the very end. .
Will the day's journey take the whole long day?
   From morn till night, my friend.

But is there for the night a resting-place?
   A roof for when the slow dark hours begin.
May not the darkness hide it from my face?
   You cannot miss that inn.

Shall I meet other wayfarers at night?
   Those who have gone before.
Then must I knock, or call when just in sight?
   They will not keep you standing at that door.

Shall I find comfort, travel-sore and weak?
   Of labour you shall find the sum.
Will there be beds for me and all who seek?
   Yea, beds for all who come.

Christina Rossetti.

THE GARDEN OF PROSERPINE.

HERE, where the world is quiet;
  Here, where all trouble seems
Dead winds' and spent waves' riot
  In doubtful dreams of dreams;
I watch the green field growing
For reaping folk and sowing,
For harvest-time and mowing,
  A sleepy world of streams.

I am tired of tears and laughter,
  And men that laugh and weep;
Of what may come hereafter
  For men that sow to reap:
I am weary of days and hours,
Blown buds of barren flowers,
Desires and dreams and powers,
  And everything but sleep.

Here life has death for neighbour,
  And far from eye or ear
Wan waves and wet winds labour,
  Weak ships and spirits steer;
They drive adrift, and whither
They wot not who make thither;
But no such winds blow hither,
  And no such things grow here.

No growth of moor or coppice,
　No heather-flower or vine,
But bloomless buds of poppies,
　Green grapes of Proserpine,
Pale beds of blowing rushes
Where no leaf blooms or blushes
Save this whereout she crushes
　For dead men deadly wine.

Pale, without name or number,
　In fruitless fields of corn,
They bow themselves and slumber
　All night till light is born;
And like a soul belated,
In hell and heaven unmated,
By cloud and mist abated
　Comes out of darkness morn.

Though one were strong as seven,
　He too with death shall dwell,
Nor wake with wings in heaven,
　Nor weep for pains in hell;
Though one were fair as roses,
His beauty clouds and closes;
And well though love reposes
　In the end it is not well.

Pale, beyond porch and portal,
　Crowned with calm leaves, she stands
Who gathers all things mortal
　With cold immortal hands;
Her languid lips are sweeter
Than love's who fears to greet her
To men that mix and meet her
　From many times and lands.

She waits for each and other,
  She waits for all men born;
Forgets the earth her mother,
  The life of fruits and corn;
And spring and seed and swallow
Take wing for her, and follow
Where summer song rings hollow
  And flowers are put to scorn.

There go the loves that wither,
  The old loves with wearier wings;
And all dead years draw thither,
  And all disastrous things;
Dead dreams of days forsaken,
Blind buds that snows have shaken,
Wild leaves that winds have taken,
  Red strays of ruined springs.

We are not sure of sorrow,
  And joy was never sure;
To-day will die to-morrow;
  Time stoops to no man's lure;
And love, grown faint and fretful,
With lips but half-regretful
Sighs, and with eyes forgetful
  Weeps that no loves endure.

From too much love of living,
  From hope and fear set free,
We thank with brief thanksgiving
  Whatever gods may be
That no life lives for ever;
That dead men rise up never;
That even the weariest river
  Winds somewhere safe to sea.

Then star nor sun shall waken,
  Nor any change of light:
Nor sound of waters shaken,
  Nor any sound or sight:
Nor wintry leaves nor vernal,
Nor days, nor things diurnal;
Only the sleep eternal
  In an eternal night.

A. C. Swinburne.

THE DEATH OF THE SUMMER.

(HENDECASYLLABICS.)

IN the month of the long decline of roses
I, beholding the summer dead before me,
Set my face to the sea and journeyed silent,
Gazing eagerly where above the sea-mark
Flame as fierce as the fervid eyes of lions
Half divided the eyelids of the sunset;
Till I heard as it were a noise of waters
Moving tremulous under feet of angels
Multitudinous, out of all the heavens;
Knew the fluttering wind, the fluttered foliage,
Shaken fitfully, full of sound and shadow;
And saw, trodden upon by noiseless angels,
Long mysterious reaches fed by moonlight,
Sweet sad straits in a soft subsiding channel,
Blown about by the lips of winds I knew not,
Winds not born in the north nor any quarter,
Winds not warm with the south nor any sunshine;
Heard between them a voice of exultation,
"Lo, the summer is dead, the sun is faded,
  Even like as a leaf the year is withered;

All the fruits of the day from all her branches
Gathered, neither is any left to gather.
All the flowers are dead, the tender blossoms
All are taken away; the season wasted,
Like an ember among the fallen ashes.
Now with light of the winter days, with moonlight,
Light of snow, and the bitter light of hoarfrost,
We bring flowers that fade not after autumn,
Pale white chaplets and crowns of latter seasons,
Fair false leaves (but the summer leaves were falser),
Woven under the eyes of stars and planets
When low light was upon the windy reaches
Where the flower of foam was blown, a lily
Dropt among the sonorous fruitless furrows
And green fields of the sea that make no pasture:
Since the winter begins, the weeping winter,
All whose flowers are tears, and round his temples
Iron blossom of frost is bound for ever."

A. C. Swinburne.

CATULLIAN HENDECASYLLABLES.

HEAR, my beloved, an old Milesian story!—
High, and embosom'd in congregated laurels,
Glimmer'd a temple upon a breezy headland;
In the dim distance amid the skyey billows
Rose a fair island; the god of flocks had placed it.
From the far shores of the bleak resounding island
Oft by the moonlight a little boat came floating,
Came to the sea-cave beneath the breezy headland,
Where amid myrtles a pathway stole in mazes
Up to the groves of the high embosom'd temple.
There in a thicket of dedicated roses,
Oft did a priestess, as lovely as a vision,
Pouring her soul to the son of Cytherea,
Pray him to hover around the slight canoe-boat,
And with invisible pilotage to guide it
Over the dusk wave, until the nightly sailor
Shivering with ecstasy sank upon her bosom.

S. T. Coleridge.

MILTON.

(ALCAICS.)

O MIGHTY mouth'd inventor of harmonies,
O skill'd to sing of Time or Eternity,
   God-gifted organ-voice of England,
      Milton, a name to resound for ages;
Whose Titan angels, Gabriel, Abdiel,
Starr'd from Jehovah's gorgeous armouries,
   Tower, as the deep-domed empyrëan
      Rings to the roar of an angel onset—

Me rather all that bowery loneliness,
The brooks of Eden mazily murmuring,
   And bloom profuse and cedar arches
      Charm, as a wanderer out in ocean
Where some refulgent sunset of India
Streams o'er a rich ambrosial ocean-isle,
   And crimson-hued the stately palmwoods
      Whisper in odorous heights of even.

A. Tennyson.

IN ARCADY.

(ELEGIACS.)

TRUNKS the forest yielded, with gums ambrosial oozing,
  Boughs with apples laden, beautiful, Hesperian—
Golden, odoriferous, perfume exhaling about them,
  Orbs in a dark umbrage luminous and radiant;
To the palate grateful, more luscious were not in Eden,
  Or in that fabled garden of Alcinoüs;
Out of a dark umbrage sounds also musical issued,
  Birds their sweet transports uttering in melody,
Thrushes clear-piping, wood-pigeons cooing, arousing
  Loudly the nightingale, loudly the sylvan echoes;
Waters transpicuous flowed under, flowed to the listening
  Ear with a soft murmur, softly soporiferous:
Nor, with ebon locks, too, there wanted, circling, attentive,
  Unto the sweet fluting, girls, of a swarthy shepherd;
Over a sunny level their flocks are lazily feeding;
  They, of Amor musing, rest in a leafy cavern.

A. H. Clough.

ODE ON A GRECIAN URN.

1.

THOU still unravish'd bride of quietness!
  Thou foster-child of Silence and slow Time,
Sylvan historian, who canst thus express
  A flowery tale more sweetly than our rhyme:
What leaf-fringed legend haunts about thy shape
    Of deities or mortals, or of both,
      In Tempe or the dales of Arcady?
    What men or gods are these? What maidens loath?
What mad pursuit? What struggle to escape?
    What pipes and timbrels? What wild ecstasy?

2.

Heard melodies are sweet, but those unheard
  Are sweeter; therefore, ye soft pipes, play on;
Not to the sensual ear, but, more endear'd,
  Pipe to the spirit ditties of no tone:
Fair youth beneath the trees, thou canst not leave
    Thy song, nor ever can those trees be bare;
      Bold Lover, never, never canst thou kiss,
    Though winning near the goal—yet, do not grieve;
She cannot fade, though thou hast not thy bliss,
    For ever wilt thou love, and she be fair!

3.

Ah, happy, happy boughs! that cannot shed
  Your leaves, nor ever bid the Spring adieu;
And happy melodist, unwearied,
  For ever piping songs for ever new;

More happy love! more happy, happy love!
  For ever warm and still to be enjoy'd,
    For ever panting and for ever young;
All breathing human passion far above,
  That leaves a heart high sorrowful and cloy'd,
    A burning forehead, and a parching tongue.

4.

Who are these coming to the sacrifice?
  To what green altar, O mysterious priest,
Lead'st thou that heifer lowing at the skies,
  And all her silken flanks with garlands drest?
What little town by river or sea-shore,
  Or mountain-built with peaceful citadel,
    Is emptied of its folk, this pious morn?
And, little town, thy streets for evermore
  Will silent be; and not a soul to tell
    Why thou art desolate, can e'er return.

5.

O Attic shape! Fair attitude! with brede
  Of marble men and maidens over-wrought,
With forest branches and the trodden weed;
  Thou, silent form! dost tease us out of thought
As doth eternity.   Cold Pastoral!
  When old age shall this generation waste,
    Thou shalt remain, in midst of other woe
Than ours, a friend to man, to whom thou say'st
"Beauty is truth, truth beauty,"—that is all
    Ye know on earth, and all ye need to know.

John Keats.

AN ANTIQUE INTAGLIO.

(Le Jeune Homme caressant sa chimère: agate rouge, trouvée près de Sorrente, rapportée au Musée de Naples.)

A BOY of eighteen years mid myrtle-boughs
  Lying love-languid on a morn of May,
Watched half asleep his goats insatiate browse
  Thin shoots of thyme and lentisk by the spray
  Of biting sea-winds bitter made and grey:
Therewith when shadows fell, his waking thought
Of love into a wondrous dream was wrought.

A woman lay beside him,—so it seemed;
  For on her marble shoulders, like a mist
Irradiate with ruddy splendour, gleamed
  Thick silken tresses; her white woman's wrist,
  Glittering with snaky gold and amethyst,
Upheld a dainty chin; and there beneath
Her twin breasts shone like pinks that lilies wreath.

What colour were her eyes I cannot tell;
  For as he gazed thereon, at times they darted
Dun rays like water in a dusky well;
  Then turned to topaz: then like rubies smarted
  With smouldering flames of passion tiger-hearted;
Then 'neath blue-veinéd lids swam soft and tender
With pleadings and shy timorous surrender.

Thus far a woman: but the breath that lifted
  Her panting breast with long melodious sighs,
Stirred o'er her neck and hair broad wings that sifted
  The perfumes of meridian Paradise;
  Dusk were they, furred like velvet, gemmed with eyes
Of such dull lustre as in isles afar
Night-flying moths spread to the summer star.

Music these pinions made—a sound and surge
  Of pines innumerous near lisping waves—
Rustlings of reeds and rushes on the verge
  Of level lakes and Naiad-haunted caves—
  Drowned whispers of a wandering stream that laves
Deep alder-boughs and tracts of ferney grass
Bordered with azure-belled campanulas.

Potent they were: for never since her birth
  With feet of woman this fair siren pressed
Sleek meadow-swards or stony ways of earth;
  But neath the milky marvel of her breast,
  Displayed in sinuous length of coil and crest,
Glittered a serpent's tail, fold over fold,
In mazy labyrinths of langour rolled.

Ah me! what fascination! what faint stars
  Of emerald and opal, with the shine
Of rubies intermingled, and dim bars
  Of twisting turquoise and pale coralline!
  What rings and rounds! what thin streaks sapphirine
Freckled that gleaming glory, like the bed
Of Eden streams with gems enamelléd!

There lurked no loathing, no soul-freezing fear,
  But luxury and love these coils between:
Faint grew the boy; the siren filled his ear
  With singing sweet as when the village-green
  Re-echoes to the tinkling tambourine,

And feet of girls aglow with laughter glance
In myriad mazy errors of the dance.

How long he dallied with delusive joy
   I know not: but thereafter nevermore
The peace of passionless slumber soothed the boy;
   For he was stricken to the very core
   With sickness of desire exceeding sore,
And through the radiance of his eyes there shone
Consuming fire too fierce to gaze upon.

He, ere he died—and they whom lips divine
   Have touched, fade flower-like and cease to be—
Bade Charicles on agate carve a sign
   Of his strange slumber: therefore can we see
   Here in the ruddy gem's transparency
The boy, the myrtle-boughs, the triple spell
Of moth and snake and white witch terrible.

J. A. Symonds.

CLEON.

"As certain also of your own poets have said"—

CLEON the poet, (from the sprinkled isles,
Lily on lily, that o'erlace the sea,
And laugh their pride when the light wave lisps "Greece")
To Protus in his Tyranny: much health!

They give thy letter to me, even now:
I read and seem as if I heard thee speak.
The master of thy galley still unlades
Gift after gift; they block my court at last
And pile themselves along its portico
Royal with sunset, like a thought of thee:
And one white she-slave from the group dispersed
Of black and white slaves, (like the chequer-work
Pavement, at once my nation's work and gift,
Now covered with this settle-down of doves)
One lyric woman, in her crocus vest
Woven of sea-wools, with her two white hands
Commends to me the strainer and the cup
Thy lip hath bettered ere it blesses mine.

Well-counselled, king, in thy munificence!
For so shall men remark, in such an act
Of love for him whose song gives life its joy,
Thy recognition of the use of life;
Nor call thy spirit barely adequate

To help on life in straight ways, broad enough
For vulgar souls, by ruling and the rest.
Thou, in the daily building of thy tower,
Whether in fierce and sudden spasms of toil,
Or through dim lulls of unapparent growth,
Or when the general work 'mid good acclaim
Climbed with the eye to cheer the architect,
Didst ne'er engage in work for mere work's sake—
Hadst ever in thy heart the luring hope
Of some eventual rest a-top of it,
Whence, all the tumult of the building hushed,
Thou first of men mightst look out to the East:
The vulgar saw thy tower, thou sawest the sun.
For this, I promise on thy festival
To pour libation, looking o'er the sea,
Making this slave narrate thy fortunes, speak
Thy great words, and describe thy royal face—
Wishing thee wholly where Zeus lives the most,
Within the eventual element of calm,

Thy letter's first requirement meets me here.
It is as thou hast heard: in one short life
I, Cleon, have effected all those things
Thou wonderingly dost enumerate.
That epos on thy hundred plates of gold
Is mine,—and also mine the little chant,
So sure to rise from every fishing-bark
When, lights at prow, the seamen haul their net.
The image of the sun-god on the phare,
Men turn from the sun's self to see, is mine;
The Pœcile, o'er-storied its whole length,
As thou didst hear, with painting, is mine too.
I know the true proportions of a man
And woman also, not observed before;
And I have written three books on the soul,
Proving absurd all written hitherto,

And putting us to ignorance again.
For music,—why, I have combined the moods,
Inventing one. In brief, all arts are mine;
Thus much the people know and recognise,
Throughout our seventeen islands.   Marvel not.
We of these latter days, with greater mind
Than our forerunners, since more composite,
Look not so great, beside their simple way,
To a judge who only sees one way at once,
One mind-point and no other at a time,—
Compares the small part of a man of us
With some whole man of the heroic age,
Great in his way—not ours, nor meant for ours.
And ours is greater, had we skill to know:
For, what we call this life of men on earth,
This sequence of the soul's achievements here,
Being, as I find much reason to conceive,
Intended to be viewed eventually
As a great whole, not analysed to parts,
But each part having reference to all,—
How shall a certain part, pronounced complete,
Endure effacement by another part?
Was the thing done?—then, what's to do again?
See, in the chequered pavement opposite,
Suppose the artist made a perfect rhomb,
And next a lozenge, then a trapezoid—
He did not overlay them, superimpose
The new upon the old and blot it out,
But laid them on at level in his work,
Making at last a picture; there it lies.
So first the perfect separate forms were made,
The portions of mankind; and after, so,
Occurred the combination of the same.
For where had been a progress, otherwise?
Mankind, made up of all the single men,—
In such a synthesis the labour ends.
Now mark me! those divine men of old time

Have reached, thou sayest well, each at one point
The outside verge that rounds our faculty;
And where they reached, who can do more than reach?
It takes but little water just to touch
At some one point the inside of a sphere,
And, as we turn the sphere, touch all the rest
In due succession: but the finer air
Which not so palpably nor obviously,
Though no less universally, can touch
The whole circumference of that emptied sphere,
Fills it more fully than the water did;
Holds thrice the weight of water in itself
Resolved into a subtler element.
And yet the vulgar call the sphere first full
Up to the visible height—and after, void;
Not knowing air's more hidden properties.
And thus our soul, misknown, cries out to Zeus
To vindicate his purpose in our life:
Why stay we on the earth unless to grow?
Long since, I imaged, wrote the fiction out,
That he or other god descended here
And, once for all, showed simultaneously
What, in its nature, never can be shown
Piecemeal or in succession:—showed, I say,
The worth both absolute and relative
Of all his children from the birth of time,
His instruments for all appointed work.
I now go on to image,—might we hear
The judgment which should give the due to each,
Show where the labour lay and where the ease,
And prove Zeus' self, the latent everywhere!
This is a dream:—but no dream, let us hope,
That years and days, the summers and the springs,
Follow each other with unwaning powers.
The grapes which dye thy wine are richer far,
Through culture, than the wild wealth of the rock;
The suave plum than the savage-tasted drupe;

The pastured honey-bee drops choicer sweet;
The flowers turn double, and the leaves turn flowers;
That young and tender crescent moon, thy slave,
Sleeping upon her robe as if on clouds,
Refines upon the women of my youth.
What, and the soul alone deteriorates?
I have not chanted verse like Homer, no—
Nor swept string like Terpander, no—nor carved
And painted men like Phidias and his friend:
I am not great as they are, point by point.
But I have entered into sympathy
With these four, running these into one soul,
Who, separate, ignored each others' arts.
Say, is it nothing that I know them all?
The wild flower was the larger; I have dashed
Rose-blood upon its petals, pricked its cup's
Honey with wine, and driven its seed to fruit,
And show a better flower if not so large:
I stand myself. Refer this to the gods
Whose gift alone it is! which, shall I dare
(All pride apart) upon the absurd pretext
That such a gift by chance lay in my hand,
Discourse of lightly or depreciate?
It might have fallen to another's hand: what then?
I pass too surely: let at least truth stay!

And next, of what thou followest on to ask.
This being with me as I declare, O king,
My works, in all these varicoloured kinds,
So done by me, accepted so by men—
Thou askest, if (my soul thus in men's hearts)
I must not be accounted to attain
The very crown and proper end of life?
Inquiring thence how, now life closeth up,
I face death with success in my right hand:
Whether I fear death less than dost thyself

The fortunate of men! "For" (writest thou)
"Thou leavest much behind, while I leave nought.
"Thy life stays in the poems men shall sing,
"The pictures men shall study; while my life,
"Complete and whole now in its power and joy,
"Dies altogether with my brain and arm,
"Is lost indeed; since, what survives' myself?
"The brazen statue to o'erlook my grave,
"Set on the promontory which I named.
"And that—some supple courtier of my heir
"Shall use its robed and sceptred arm, perhaps,
"To fix the rope to, which best drags it down.
"I go then: triumph thou, who dost not go!"

  Nay, thou art worthy of hearing my whole mind.
Is this apparent, when thou turn'st to muse
Upon the scheme of earth and man in chief,
That admiration grows as knowledge grows?
That imperfection means perfection hid,
Reserved in part, to grace the after-time?
If, in the morning of philosophy,
Ere aught had been recorded, nay perceived,
Thou, with the light now in thee, couldst have looked
On all earth's tenantry, from worm to bird,
Ere man, her last, appeared upon the stage—
Thou wouldst have seen them perfect, and deduced
The perfectness of others yet unseen.
Conceding which,—had Zeus then questioned thee
"Shall I go on a step, improve on this,
"Do more for visible creatures than is done?"
Thou wouldst have answered, "Ay, by making each
"Grow conscious in himself—by that alone.
"All's perfect else: the shell sucks fast the rock,
"The fish strikes through the sea, the snake both swims
"And slides, forth range the beasts, the birds take flight,

"Till life's mechanics can no further go—
"And all this joy in natural life is put
"Like fire from off thy finger into each,
"So exquisitely perfect is the same.
"But 'tis pure fire, and they mere matter are;
"It has them, not they it; and so I choose
"For man, thy last premeditated work
"(If I might add a glory to the scheme)
"That a third thing should stand apart from both,
"A quality arise within his soul,
"Which, intro-active, made to supervise
"And feel the force it has, may view itself,
"And so be happy." Man might live at first
The animal life: but is there nothing more?
In due time, let him critically learn
How he lives; and, the more he gets to know
Of his own life's adaptabilities,
The more joy-giving will his life become.
Thus man, who hath this quality, is best.

But thou, king, hadst more reasonably said:
"Let progress end at once,—man make no step
"Beyond the natural man, the better beast,
"Using his senses, not the sense of sense."
In man there's failure, only since he left
The lower and inconscious forms of life.
We called it an advance, the rendering plain
Man's spirit might grow conscious of man's life,
And, by new lore so added to the old,
Take each step higher over the brute's head.
Thus grew the only life, the pleasure-house,
Watch-tower and treasure-fortress of the soul,
Which whole surrounding flats of natural life
Seemed only fit to yield subsistence to;
A tower that crowns a country. But alas,

The soul now climbs it just to perish there!
For thence we have discovered ('tis no dream—
We know this, which we had not else perceived)
That there's a world of capability
For joy, spread round about us, meant for us,
Inviting us; and still the soul craves all,
And still the flesh replies, "Take no jot more
"Than ere thou clombst the tower to look abroad!
"Nay, so much less as that fatigue has brought
"Deduction to it." We struggle fain to enlarge
Our bounded physical recipiency,
Increase our power, supply fresh oil to life,
Repair the waste of age and sickness: no,
It skills not! life's inadequate to joy,
As the soul sees joy, tempting life to take.
They praise a fountain in my garden here
Wherein a Naiad sends the water-bow
Thin from her tube; she smiles to see it rise.
What if I told her, it is just a thread
From that great river which the hills shut up,
And mock her with my leave to take the same?
The artificer has given her one small tube
Past power to widen or exchange—what boots
To know she might spout oceans if she could?
She cannot lift beyond her first thin thread:
And so a man can use but a man's joy
While he sees God's. Is it for Zeus to boast
"See, man, how happy I live, and despair—
"That I may be still happier—for thy use!"
If this were so, we could not thank our Lord,
As hearts beat on to doing: 'tis not so—
Malice it is not. Is it carelessness?
Still, no. If care—where is the sign? I ask,
And get no answer, and agree in sum,
O king, with thy profound discouragement,
Who seest the wider but to sigh the more.
Most progress is most failure: thou sayest well.

The last point now:—thou dost except a case—
Holding joy not impossible to one
With artist-gifts—to such a man as I
Who leave behind me living works indeed;
For, such a poem, such a painting lives.
What! dost thou verily trip upon a word,
Confound the accurate view of what joy is
(Caught somewhat clearer by my eyes than thine)
With feeling joy! confound the knowing how
And showing how to live (my faculty)
With actually living!—Otherwise
Where is the artist's vantage o'er the king!
Because in my great epos I display
How divers men young, strong, fair, wise, can act—
Is this as though I acted! if I paint,
Carve the young Phœbus, am I therefore young!
Methinks I'm older that I bowed myself
The many years of pain that taught me art!
Indeed, to know is something, and to prove
How all this beauty might be enjoyed, is more:
But, knowing nought, to enjoy is something too.
Yon rower, with the moulded muscles there,
Lowering the sail, is nearer it than I.
I can write love-odes: thy fair slave's an ode.
I get to sing of love, when grown too grey
For being beloved: she turns to that young man,
The muscles all a-ripple on his back.
I know the joy of kingship: well, thou art king!

    "But," sayest thou—(and I marvel, I repeat,
To find thee tripping on a mere word) "what
"Thou writest, paintest, stays; that does not die:
"Sappho survives, because we sing her songs,
"And Æschylus, because we read his plays!"
Why, if they live still, let them come and take
Thy slave in my despite, drink from thy cup,

Speak in my place. Thou diest while I survive?
Say rather that my fate is deadlier still,
In this, that every day my sense of joy
Grows more acute, my soul (intensified
By power and insight) more enlarged, more keen;
While every day my hairs fall more and more,
My hand shakes, and the heavy years increase—
The horror quickening still from year to year,
The consummation coming past escape,
When I shall know most, and yet least enjoy—
When all my works wherein I prove my worth,
Being present still to mock me in men's mouths,
Alive still, in the phrase of such as thou,
I—I—the feeling, thinking, acting man,
The man who loved his life so over-much,
Shall sleep in my urn. It is so horrible,
I dare at times imagine to my need
Some future state revealed to us by Zeus,
Unlimited in capability
For joy, as this is in desire for joy,
To seek which, the joy-hunger forces us,
That, stung by straitness of our life—made strait
On purpose to make prized the life at large—
Freed by the throbbing impulse we call death,
We burst there as the worm into the fly,
Who, while a worm still, wants his wings. But no!
Zeus has not yet revealed it; and alas,
He must have done so, were it possible!

    Live long and happy, and in that thought die,
Glad for what was! Farewell. And for the rest,
I cannot tell thy messenger aright
Where to deliver what he bears of thine
To one called Paulus; we have heard his fame
Indeed, if Christus be not one with him—
I know not, nor am troubled much to know.

Thou canst not think a mere barbarian Jew,
As Paulus proves to be, one circumcised,
Hath access to a secret shut from us?
Thou wrongest our philosophy, O king,
In stooping to inquire of such an one,
As if his answer could impose at all!
He writeth, doth he? well, and he may write.
Oh, the Jew findeth scholars! certain slaves
Who touched on this same isle, preached him and Christ;
And (as I gathered from a bystander)
Their doctrine could be held by no sane man.

R. Browning.

THE BLESSÈD DAMOZEL.

THE blessèd damozel leaned out
  From the gold bar of Heaven;
Her eyes were deeper than the depth
  Of waters stilled at even;
She had three lilies in her hand,
  And the stars in her hair were seven.

Her robe, ungirt from clasp to hem,
  No wrought flowers did adorn,
But a white rose of Mary's gift,
  For service meetly worn;
Her hair that lay along her back
  Was yellow like ripe corn.

Her seemed she scarce had been a day
  One of God's choristers;
The wonder was not yet quite gone
  From that still look of hers;
Albeit, to them she left, her day
  Had counted as ten years.

(To one, it is ten years of years.
  . . . . Yet now, and in this place,
Surely she leaned o'er me—her hair
  Fell all about my face . . . . .
Nothing: the autumn fall of leaves.
  The whole year sets apace.)

It was the rampart of God's House
   That she was standing on;
By God built over the sheer depth
   The which is Space begun;
So high, that looking downward thence
   She scarce could see the sun.

It lies in Heaven, across the flood
   Of ether, as a bridge.
Beneath, the tides of day and night
   With flame and darkness ridge
The void, as low as where this earth
   Spins like a fretful midge.

Around her, lovers newly met
   Mid deathless love's acclaims
Spake evermore among themselves
   Their rapturous new names;
And the souls mounting up to God
   Went by her like thin flames.

And still she bowed herself and stooped
   Out of the circling charm;
Until her bosom must have made
   The bar she leaned on warm,
And the lilies lay as half asleep
   Along her bended arm.

From the fixed place of Heaven she saw
   Time like a pulse shake fierce
Through all the worlds. Her gaze still strove
   Within the gulf to pierce
Its path; and now she spoke as when
   The stars sang in their spheres.

The sun was gone now; the curled moon
   Was like a little feather
Fluttering far down the gulf; and now
   She spoke through the still weather.
Her voice was like the voice the stars
   Had when they sang together.

(Ah sweet! Even now, in that bird's song,
   Strove not her accents there,
Fain to be hearkened? When those bells
   Possessed the mid-day air,
Strove not her steps to reach my side
   Down all the echoing stair?)

"I wish that he were come to me,
   For he will come," she said.
"Have I not prayed in Heaven?—on earth,
   Lord, Lord, has he not pray'd?
Are not two prayers a perfect strength?
   And shall I feel afraid?

"When round his head the aureole clings,
   And he is clothed in white,
I'll take his hand and go with him
   To the deep wells of light;
We will step down as to a stream,
   And bathe there in God's sight.

"We two will stand beside that shrine,
   Occult, witheld, untrod,
Whose lamps are stirred continually
   With prayer sent up to God;
And see our old prayers, granted, melt
   Each like a little cloud.

"We two will lie i' the shadow of
    That living mystic tree
Within whose secret growth the Dove
    Is sometimes felt to be,
While every leaf that His plumes touch
    Saith His Name audibly.

"And I myself will teach to him,
    I myself, lying so,
The songs I sing here; which his voice
    Shall pause in, hushed and slow,
And find some knowledge at each pause,
    Or some new thing to know."

(Alas! We two, we two, thou say'st!
    Yea, one wast thou with me
That once of old. But shall God lift
    To endless unity
The soul whose likeness with thy soul
    Was but its love for thee?)

"We two," she said, "will seek the groves
    Where the lady Mary is,
With her five hand-maidens, whose names
    Are five sweet symphonies,
Cecily, Gertrude, Magdalen,
    Margaret and Rosalys.

"Circlewise sit they, with bound locks
    And foreheads garlanded;
Into the fine cloth white like flame
    Weaving the golden thread,
To fashion the birth-robes for them
    Who are just born, being dead.

"He shall fear, haply, and be dumb:
　　Then will I lay my cheek
To his, and tell about our love,
　　Not once abashed or weak:
And the dear Mother will approve
　　My pride, and let me speak.

"Herself shall bring us, hand in hand,
　　To Him round whom all souls
Kneel, the clear-ranged unnumbered heads
　　Bowed with their aureoles:
And angels meeting us shall sing
　　To their citherns and citoles.

"There will I ask of Christ the Lord
　　Thus much for him and me:—
Only to live as once on earth
　　With Love,—only to be
As then awhile, for ever now
　　Together, I and he."

She gazed and listened and then said,
　　Less sad of speech than mild,—
"All this is when he comes." She ceased.
　　The light thrilled towards her, fill'd
With angels in strong level flight.
　　Her eyes prayed, and she smil'd.

(I saw her smile.) But soon their path
　　Was vague in distant spheres;
And then she cast her arms along
　　The golden barriers,
And laid her face between her hands,
　　And wept. (I heard her tears.)

D. G. Rossetti.

THE SEA LIMITS.

CONSIDER the sea's listless chime;
  Time's self it is, made audible,—
  The murmur of the earth's own shell.
Secret continuance sublime
  Is the sea's end: our sight may pass
  No furlong further. Since time was,
This sound hath told the lapse of time.

No quiet, which is death's,—it hath
  The mournfulness of ancient life,
  Enduring always at dull strife.
As the world's heart of rest and wrath,
  Its painful pulse is in the sands.
  Last utterly, the whole sky stands,
Grey and not known, along its path.

Listen alone beside the sea,
  Listen alone among the woods;
  Those voices of twin solitudes
Shall have one sound alike to thee:
  Hark where the murmurs of thronged men
  Surge and sink back and surge again,—
Still the one voice of wave and tree.

Gather a shell from the strown beach
  And listen at its lips: they sigh
  The same desire and mystery,
The echo of the whole sea's speech.
  And all mankind is thus at heart:
  Not anything but what thou art:
And Earth, Sea, Man, are all in each.

                              D. G. Rossetti.

NOTES.

Page 3. "JOHN ANDERSON"—*R. Burns.* Line 1. "*jo,*" sweetheart. L. 4. *brent,* smooth, bright. L. 7. "*pow*" pole, or head.

Page 4. "OH, WERT THOU IN THE CAULD BLAST" Line 3. "*airt*" quarter of the heavens. L. 7. "*bield*" shelter.

Page 6. "MY JEAN"—Line 5. "*row*" roll. L. 6. Verse 2. "*shaw,*" a small wood in a hollow, a copse. The four short songs by Burns with which the Second Part opens may be cited as almost faultless models of the class of poetry they represent.

Page 9. "HIGHLAND MARY"—*R. Burns.* Line 4. Verse 1. "*Drumlie,*" muddy. L. 1. V. 2. "*birk*" birch.

Page 12. "THE PROMISE OF CHILDHOOD." Ibid. Line 4. Verse 5. "*tents*" guards, tends.

Page 18. "NIGHT AND DEATH"—*J. B. White.* Coleridge pronounced this sonnet "the best in the English language," and L. Hunt adds that "in point of *thought,* it stands supreme, perhaps above all in any language." Our admiration is almost exceeded by our wonder when it is remembered that the author was born and brought up in Spain, was no longer young when he came to England, and then spoke English like a foreigner.

Page 20. "THE IDEAL HERMITAGE"—*W. Wordsworth.* Line 13. "*thorp*" a hamlet. Ibid. "*vill*" village.

Page 22. "FOR A GROTTO." This little-known and seldom-quoted "*Inscription for a grotto*" is exquisitely Greek in sentiment, and might have been written by Theocritus.

Page 23. "ODE TO CONTEMPLATION"—*H. K. White.* An undeniable imitation of the "Penseroso" of Milton; but a charming poem. Line 2. "*Lapponian*" Laplandish. L. 29. "*Singing of one that died for love*" a delicious touch, that puts the whole ballad before us in a line.

Page 27. "KUBLA KHAN"—*S. T. Coleridge.* Of this poem, the writer himself narrates how it came to him in a dream, as he was sleeping one day in his chair. Waking, he seized the pen and wrote thus far from memory, when, being interrupted by a visitor, he lost the frail thread of recollection and never remembered the rest. The dream was suggested by a passage in Purchas's travels, over which he had fallen asleep.

Page 25. "THE ISLES OF GREECE"—*Lord Byron*. Line 5. Verse 3. "*the Persians' grave*," the tumulus raised over the Persian slain. L. 1. Verse 4. "*a king sat on the rocky brow*" Xerxes. L. 1. Verse 10. "*You have the Pyrrhic dance*" Dodwell, in his Tour in Greece, relates that the Greek mountaineers still preserved a kind of Pyrrhic dance which they performed, armed with swords and muskets. L. 5. Verse 10. "*the letters Cadmus gave*" Cadmus, a Phœnician prince, said to have introduced into Greece an alphabet of 16 letters from either Phœnicia or Egypt. L. 6. Verse 13. "*Heracleidan*" the descendants of Hercules. L. 1. Verse 16. "*Sunium's marbled steep*"—the promontory of Sunium forms the S. extremity of Attica, and is crowned by the noble ruins of a splendid temple to Athena. This poem and the two which follow it strike the same note of sympathy with the struggle for Greek liberty that possessed Europe from commencement of the war of independance in 1821 till the evacuation of the Morea by the Turks in 1828.

Page 35. "THE BOWL OF LIBERTY"—*Mrs. Hemans*. The Platæans held an anniversary solemnity to the memory of those who fell fighting for their country's liberty. At break of day, on the 16th of the month called Mamacterion, they went out in procession to the sepulchres—a trumpeter going first, then three chariots laden with garlands and myrrh; then a black bull for the sacrifice; then a body of free-born youth bearing jars of wine, oil, and precious ointments; lastly the chief magistrate of Platæa clothed in purple. Arrived at the sepulchres, the magistrate sprinkled and anointed them, sacrificed the bull, and in a loud voice invited the Souls of the Heroes to this funereal feast. He then filled a bowl of wine, and said "I drink to those who lost their lives for the liberty of Greece." Plutarch states that these august and ancient ceremonies were observed in his day.

Page 41. "LOVE LEFT SORROWING"—*W. Wordsworth*—a poem peculiarly Wordsworthian; abounding in characteristic beauties of feeling and style, and not without that touch of simplicity, almost approaching to grotesqueness, which stamps certain of the poet's rural pieces. We seem to see a sort of gentle modern Polyphemus in the big man, able to dance "equipped from head to foot in iron mail."

Page 57. "BANNOCKBURN"—*R. Burns*. The army of Edward II. was totally routed at Bannockburn near Stirling, by Robert Bruce, King of Scots, June 24th 1314.

Page 59. "THE BATTLE OF IVRY"—*Lord Macaulay*. Henry IV. defeated the League army at Ivry, near Evreux, March 14th A.D. 1590.

Page 62. "HOHENLINDEN"—*T. Campbell*. The Austrians, commanded by the Archduke John, were defeated at Hohenlinden by the French and Bavarian army under Moreau, Dec. 3th A.D. 1800.

Page 63. "PIBROCH OF DONALD DHU"—*Sir W. Scott*. Founded on a very ancient Pibroch supposed to relate to the expedition of Donald Balloch who, in 1431, at the head of a greatly inferior force defeated and routed the Earls of Mar and Caithness at Inverlochy.

Page 65. "CORONACH." Ibid. The coronach of the Highlanders, like the *ululatus* of the Romans and the *ululoo* of the Irish, was a wild cry of lament tion raised over a dead body. Line 1. Verse 3. "correi" covert on the hill side. L. 2. ibid. "*cumber*" trouble. L. 3. ibid. "foray" fight.

Page 66. "THE BURIAL OF SIR JOHN MOORE"—*C. Wolfe.* The battle of Corunna was fought (N.W. Spain) between 15000 English under Sir J. Moore and 20,000 French, Jan. 16th 1809. The English achieved a complete victory, but at the cost of immense losses, among which the greatest was that of Sir J. Moore.

Page 70. "AFTER BLENHEIM"—*R. Southey.* A masterpiece of simple and pathetic irony.

Page 72. "OZYMANDIAS OF EGYPT"—*P. B. Shelley.* Ozymandias and Sesostris are names erroneously given by the Greeks to Rameses II. surnamed the Great, the most illustrious conqueror, temple-builder and art-patron of Egyptian history. This fine sonnet could scarcely have been more beautiful or impressive if written under the influence of a Theban sky; but it would certainly have been more true to facts if the writer had ever visited in person the scene he so poetically describes. The great fallen statue (greatest of all known monolithic colossi) lies shattered out of form and recognition at the SW. side of the ruins of the Memnonium, on the edge of the cultivated land and close against the foot of the Theban mountains. The legs do not stand; they are split into innumerable fragments, and lie in heaped-up ruin. The desert-sands do not surround them. And the face of the statue is wholly gone, having been sawn away for millstones by the Arabs any time within the last two or three hundred years.

Page 73. "THE NILE"—*L. Hunt.* Take it altogether, this is perhaps the finest poem that Hunt ever wrote; the second line is absolutely perfect. Line 8. "*the laughing queen that caught the world's great hands.*" Cleopatra, who succeeded in captivating both Antony and Cæsar.

Page 75. "ROMAN ANTIQUITIES DISCOVERED"—*W. Wordsworth.* Line 12. "*the Wolf, whose suckling Twins*" &c. Romulus and Remus, fabled to have been suckled by a wolf.

Page 77. "FANCY IN NUBIBUS"—*S. T. Coleridge.* Line 11. "*that blind bard*" Homer was supposed by the ancient to have been born at Chios, though several other places claimed the honour of his birth.

Page 80. "THE MEMORY OF GREAT POETS"—*T. Hood.* Might have been written by Charles Lamb, for the fine Elizabethan flavour of the style.

Page 81. "THE WORLD OF BOOKS"—*W. Wordsworth.*—Observe the little touch of personal information in the two last lines. It is pleasant to know that Desdemona and the Una of Spenser were his two favorite ideals.

Page 83. "ODE TO THE WEST WIND"—*P.B. Shelley.* Line 21. "*Mænad*" —a Bacchante, or wild Nymph attendant on Bacchus. Had Shelley left nothing but this magnificent Ode, it would have been enough to vindicate his claim to the rank of a great poet.

Page 91. "COME DOWN, O MAID"—*A. Tennyson.* Perhaps the most beautiful and splendid of all his shorter poems.

Page 92. "CHORAL HYMN TO ARTEMIS"—*A. C. Swinburne.* Line 6. Verse 1. "*Itylus*" see note to Barnefield's "nightingale." Notes to ELDER ENGLISH POETS (First Series), p. 277. L. 6. Verse 5. "*the oat is heard above the lyre*" i. e. it is the season for the piping of shepherds, rather than for the singing of bards in palace-halls. L. 4. Verse 6. "*Bassarid*" a Bacchante.

Page 94. "Hymn of Pan"—*P. B. Shelley.* Line 11. "*old Tmolus,*" a famous mountain in Lydia. L. 26. "the dædal earth" i. e. the world in the mythic time of Dædalus; the archaic period, when architecture and the arts were in their infancy. L. 27. "the giant wars," the wars of the Titans against Zeus. L. 30. "Mænalus" a mountain in Arcadia, and the favorite haunt of Pan.

Page 97. "Persephone"—*J. Ingelow.* Persephone in the Greek for Proserpina. Persephone, the daughter of Demeter (Ceres), was carried off by Pluto while gathering flowers with her maidens in the vale of Enna. Having obtained her dread lord's permission to visit her mother, she returned to the upper world; but having eaten the pomegranate seed in Hades, was constrained to return to the lower world again, where she reigns Queen of the shades.

Page 101. "The Old Familiar Faces"—*C. Lamb.* One of the most simple, pathetic, and original poems in any language.

Page 107. "Dirge"—*T. Lovell Beddoes.* A poet little known to general readers; born near Bristol A.D. 1803; died in Basle, Jan. 26th, 1849. His poems were published by Pickering, in two volumes, in 1851. This Dirge is from "Death's Jest Book," a wild dramatic poem full of strange quaint imagery, and rare beauty of thought. Beddoes was, so to say, saturated with the spirit of the Elizabethan Dramatists, and cast his poetry for the most part into Elizabethan forms.

Page 109. "The Bridge of Sighs"—*T. Hood.* Westminster Bridge, whence many "unfortunates" used to commit suicide by throwing themselves into the Thames at the time this beautiful and pitiful poem was written.

Page 114. "After Death"—*E. A. Poe.* A poem as subtle and tender in feeling as it is novel in conception.

Page 119. "Intimations of Immortality"—*W. Wordsworth.* The genius of Wordsworth never rose to a loftier height than in this noble Ode.

Page 132. "The Daffodils." Ibid.—This poem and the one by Miss Ingelow which follows it, are delightful as showing the kind of pleasurable philosophy the poets derive from the contemplation of natural objects.

Page 135. "To a Skylark"—*P. B. Shelley.* Leigh Hunt, with admirable critical insight, says of this exquisite Ode, "it is like the bird it sings—enthusiastic, enchanting, profuse, continuous, and alone—small, but filling the heavens."

Page 139. "Ode to a Nightingale"—*J. Keats.* Line 6. Verse 2. "*Hippocrene*" a fountain in mount Helicon sacred to the muses, said to have been struck from the rock by a blow from the hoof of Pegasus. This poem was written at a time when the poet had his mortal illness upon him. "Never was the voice of Death sweeter." L. Hunt.

Page 142. "To the Cuckoo"—*W. Wordsworth.* Of this poem Mr. Palgrave says that it has "an exaltation and a glory, joined with an exquisiteness of expression, which place it in the highest rank among the many masterpieces of its illustrious author." Notes to *Golden Treasury.*

Page 145. "Itylus"—*A. C. Swinburne.* See note, as before, to Barnefield's poem on the Nightingale. Notes to Elder Poets, First Series, p. 277.

Page 151. CHRISTMAS CAROL."—*W. Morris.* Line 3. Verse 5. *"Hap"* good fortune L. 1. Verse 6. *"bent,"* a shed; literally a lean-to. L. 3. Verse 7. *"teen"* trouble. L. 3. Verse 12. *"nowell"* a cry of joy raised at Christmas in mediæval times, for the birth of the Saviour; the word is from the old Norman French, and survives in the modern *Noel.*

Page 155. "AFTER RAIN"—*W. Wordsworth.* Observe the extraordinary vivacity of this little poem, as of all things brightened, refreshed, and stirring.

Page 156. "MENIE"—*R. Burns.* Line 2. Verse 3. *"tentie"* cautious. L. 1. Verse 5. *"steeks"* shuts. Ibid. *"slap,"* gate.

Page 157. "THE PRIDE OF YOUTH"—*Sir W. Scott.* "Scott has given us nothing more complete and lovely than this little song, which unites simplicity and dramatic power to a wild-wood music of the rarest quality." Palgrave. Line 1. Verse 1. *"Maisie,"* Mary.

Page 158. "O WERE MY LOVE YON LILAC FAIR"—*R. Burns.* This delicious little love-song, and *"The Miller's Daughter"* which follows it, strike the same note of simple passion. It is hard to say which is the more lovely and natural. The first, for moderaness, might have been written yesterday; and both, for universality, might be as old as love itself.

Page 166. "EVENING"—*W. S. Landor.* Though a great wit, a great thinker, a great Hellenist, rather than a great poet, Landor has written some verses distinguished by singular transparency of style and elevation of thought. This isolated fragment of English landscape-painting might, for clearness of observation, fidelity, and simplicity, have been written by Wordsworth.

Page 170. "HYMN TO THE NIGHT"—*H. W. Longfellow.* Line 1. Verse 6. *"Orestes-like"* Orestes was the son of Agamemnon and Clytemnestra. Hounded on from land to land by the Erinnyes of his mother (whom he had slain in vengeance for her complicity in the murder of his father) he found "peace" and a refuge at last under the protection of Athena at Athens.

Page 173. "IN THE STORM"—*Hon. Mrs. Norton.* This poem, privately printed, is here given by special permission of the late lamented author.

Page 177. "AMERICA TO GREAT BRITAIN"—*W. Allston.* The writer of this hearty and spirited poem was a painter in the grand style, and greater as a painter than as a poet. Mrs. Jameson says in her memoir of him, that "in Washington Allston, America lost her third great man. What Washington was as a statesman and Channing as a moralist, that was Allston as an artist."

Page 179. "THE ARMADA"—*Lord Macaulay* — printed among the author's poetical works as "a fragment." It commemorates the signal catastrophe that brought the second war of Elizabeth's reign to a summary conclusion, when the Invincible Armada, having been chased northwards by the English fleet which numbered about 30 ships to 136, was overtaken by terrific storms and wrecked off the coasts of Scotland and Ireland (A.D. 1588). Line 7. *"Aurigny's isle"* the isle of Alderney. L. 23. *"the Picard field"* the battle of Crécy; the site of this famous fight, now included in the Departement of the Somme, was then in the Province of Picardy.

Page 184. "THE BATTLE OF THE BALTIC"—*T. Campbell* — known in history as the battle of Copenhagen; and fought off Copenhagen, April 2nd

1801, Lord Nelson commanding the British fleet. Captain Riou was justly styled "the gallant and good," by Nelson in his despatches.

Page 187. "THE CHARGE OF THE LIGHT BRIGADE"—*A. Tennyson*. The famous "death Charge" led by Lord Cardigan at the head of six hundred light cavalry, battle of Balaklava, Oct. 25th, 1854.

Page 189. "BARBARA FRITCHIE"—*J. G. Whittier*. This fine poem is founded on a noble incident of the American Civil War.

Page 195. "THE PRIDE OF WORTH"—*R. Burns*. Line 1. Verse 3. "*birkie*" a shallow conceited fellow. L. 4. Verse 3. "*coof*" blockhead. L. 2. Verse 2. "*Hoddin-grey*" home-made cloth of coarse quality. L. 4. Verse 5. "*bear the gree*"—be victor.

Page 196. "GOLD"—*T. Hood*. From the poem of Miss Kilmansegg.

Page 219. "THE LONG WHITE SEAM"—*J. Ingelow*. This poem, not yet included in any edition of her works, is here given by kind permission of the author.

Page 221. "TO A LADY WITH A GUITAR"—*P. B. Shelley*. Line 24. "*her interlunar swoon;*" the time when the moon is invisible from our Earth's surface. A very fanciful and beautiful poem. See note to a sonnet by W. Drummond entitled "to his Lute." Part 1. Notes to THE ELDER ENGLISH POETS (First Series) p. 278.

Page 226. "THE BELFRY OF BRUGES"—*H. W. Longfellow*. Line 19. Verse 10. "*all the Foresters of Flanders*" the title of Foresters was given to the early Governors of Flanders, appointed by the kings of France. L. 22. Verse 11. "*Stately dames, like queens attended*."—When Philippe-le-Bel, king of France, visited Flanders with his queen, she was so astonished at the magnificence of the dames of Bruges, that she exclaimed,—"Je croyais être seule reine ici, mais il paraît que ceux de Flandre qui se trouvent dans nos prisons sont tous des princes, car leurs femmes sont habillées comme des princesses et des reines." L. 22. "*the Fleece of Gold*" Phillippe of Burgundy called Le Bon, married Isabella of Portugal, January 10th, 1430, and on the same day instituted the famous order of the Golden Fleece. L. 26. Verse 13. "*the gentle Mary*" Marie de Valois, Duchess of Burgundy, married by proxy, with all the curious ceremonies of the period, to the Archduke Maximilian: the same who, being imprisoned by the revolted burghers of Bruges, was by them compelled to kneel down in the public square and solemnly swear that he would not take vengeance upon them for their rebellion. L. 30. Verse 15. "*The bloody battle of the Spurs of Gold*."—"This battle, the most memorable in Flemish history, was fought under the walls of Courtray, on the 11th of July, 1302, between the French and the Flemings, the former commanded by Robert, Comte d'Artois, and the latter by Guillaume de Juliers, and Jean, Comte de Namur. The French army was completely routed, with a loss of twenty thousand infantry and seven thousand cavalry; among whom were sixty-three princes, dukes, and counts, seven hundred lords-banneret, and eleven hundred noblemen. The flower of the French nobility perished on that day, to which history has given the name of the *Journée des Eperons d'Or*, from the great number of golden spurs found on the field of battle. Seven hundred of them were hung up as a trophy in the church of Notre Dame de Courtray; and, as the cavaliers of that day wore but a single spur each, these vouched to God for the violent and bloody death of seven hundred of his creatures." — *Notes to Longfellow's poems.* L. 31. Verse 16. "*Saw the fight at Minnewater.*"—"When the inhabitants of Bruges were digging a canal at Minnewater, to bring the waters of the Lys from Deynze to their city, they were attacked and routed by the citizens of Ghent, whose commerce would have been much injured by the canal. They were led by Jean Lyons, captain of a military company at Ghent, called the *Chaperons Blancs.*"—*Ibid.* L. 32. Verse 18. "*The Golden Dragon's nest.*"—The Golden Dragon, taken from the church of St. Sophia, at Constantinople, in one of the Crusades, and placed on the belfry of Bruges, was afterwards transported to Ghent by Philip van Artevelde, and still adorns the belfry of that city. The inscription on the alarm bell at Ghent is, "*Mynen naem is Roland; als ik klep is er brand, and als ik luy is er victorie in het land.*" My name is Roland; when I toll there is fire, and when I ring there is victory in the land."—*Ibid.*

Page 240. "THE STORM"—*R. Buchanan.* This grand poem has been abridged by the author, expressly for the present collection.

Page 260. "THE RECOLLECTION"—*P. B. Shelley.* Line 9. "the pine-forest that skirts the ocean's foam"—the famous pine-forest of Ravenna, which he had visited with Lord Byron the year before this poem was written. There are not many "giants" left now, nor indeed many pines that we can feel sure are old enough to have witnessed his presence.

Page 264. "A PARTING IN DREAMLAND"—*J. A. Symonds.* Line 2. "Lethe" a river in the lower world at which the shades of the departed were wont to drink, thenceforth forgetting all that they had said and done in the life past away. Those who love to systematize these pathetic and beautiful myths, see in Lethe's gift of oblivion the forgetfulness of Death. L. 5. "*Nepenthe*" a drug supposed to drive away pain; probably opium or hemp.

Page 274. "AUTUMN"—*H. W. Longfellow.* Line 3. "*silks of Samarcand*" Samarcand was the ancient capital of Turkestan, and has still some fine bazaars, but its trade has gone over for the most part to Bokhara, the modern city.

Page 278. "IN SAN LORENZO"—*A. C. Swinburne.* Line 1. "O slumbering Night." The famous statue of sleeping Night, on the tomb of Giuliano de' Medici, by Michael Angelo, in the Medici Chapel of San Lorenzo, Florence. The poet supposes the dawn of Italian liberty to be at hand—as indeed it was, when this fine sonnet was written.

Page 280. "FOR TITIAN"—*W. Morris.* With two or three exceptions only (as in the passages selected from the "Deserted Village," see Elder English Poets (First Series) A RURAL PICTURE p. 203; and certain strophes of "In Memoriam") these stanzas from "The Lady of the Land" will be seen to be a departure from the rule by which the Editor has been guided in the compilation of this book. Short poems complete in themselves have almost invariably been given, and extracts from long poems, scrupulously avoided. In the present instance, however, such departure was found to be unavoidable; for Mr. Morris's poems are all too long for insertion here, and yet some fit sample of his musical and richly-coloured style was felt to be necessary. The responsibility of giving a title to the extract devolves upon the Editor, who begs indulgence for it.

Page 281. "SONG"—*T. L. Beddoes.* This drinking song is grandly conceived. One can fancy some mighty Homeric hero calling thus upon Etna to become a wine-cloud, and rain into his cup.

Page 285. "YOUTH AND AGE"—*S. T. Coleridge.* "This is one of the most perfect poems for style, feeling and everything, that ever was written." L. Hunt. This *"and everything"* is charming.

Page 289. "THE GARDEN OF PROSERPINE"—*A. C. Swinburne.* This beautiful weird poem, in a metre new to English verse, is apparently sung by some shade in Hades. For the legend of Proserpine, or Persephone, see Note to Miss Ingelow's "Persephone," page 322.

Page 294. "CATULLIAN HENDECASYLLABLES"—*S. T. Coleridge.* Line 5. *"the god of flocks"*—Apollo, νόμιος θεός. Apollo is rarely treated of in this character by Homer, but chiefly by the later poets, and in the Thessalian myth wherein he tends the flocks of Admetus. L. 13. *"the son of Cytherea"* Cytherea was the Aphrodite especially worshipped in the island of Cythera; and it was off the coast of this island that she was fabled to have risen from the sea-foam. Eros, the God of Love, was the son of Cytherea and Ares.

Page 295. "MILTON"—*A. Tennyson.* This poem is interesting alike for its magnificent grasp of language, and for the declaration of individual taste which it conveys.

Page 296. "IN ARCADY"—*A. H. Clough.* Line 6. *"that fabled garden of Alcinoüs."* Alcinoüs was king of the Phæacians in the isle of Scheria. For the description of his palace and gardens see the Odyssey of Homer. Book VII.

Page 297. "ODE ON A GRECIAN URN"—*J. Keats.* We do not know in the whole field of English poetry a more exquisite piece of fancy than this, which supposes a moment of early Greek life, with its buoyant gaiety and all its simple incidents, transferred to the surface of the Urn and there arrested for ever.

Page 299. "AN ANTIQUE INTAGLIO"—*J. A. Symonds.* Of this poem, it is unnecessary to observe that the legend and the intaglio alike exist only in the poet's imagination.

Page 302. "CLEON"—*R. Browning.* Line 53. Page 303. *"the Pœcile"* i. e. a variegated, or brightly decorated place painted with many colours. There was at Athens a gallery adorned with paintings, called "the Pœcile;" hence other similar galleries came generally to be so styled. Cleon, having such a gallery in his island, painted by himself, gives it therefore this name. There is also a rock on the coast of Cilicia called *The Pœcile,* on which have of late years been discovered the ruins of a Roman town built during the reigns of Valentinian, Valens and Gratian. L. 132. Page 305. *"Savage-tasted drupe"* an over-ripe, wrinkled olive. L. 140. Page 306. *"Terpander"* a native of Antissa in Lesbos, who flourished somewhere between BC. 700 and 650. He is reported to have first reduced Greek music to a system; to have added three strings to the lyre, and to have been the first victor in the musical contests at the Festival of the Carnëa. L. 141. *"Phidias"* the greatest sculptor of ancient Greece, under whose superintendence the Parthenon and Propylæa

built. and whose masterpieces were supposed to be the cryselephantine
ies of Athena at Athens, and of Jupiter at Olympia.
Page 313. "THE BLESSÈD DAMOSEL"—*D. G. Rossetti.* For pathos, and
y, and mediævalism of the most exquisite kind, this poem may fitly be
ared with the missal-paintings of Fra Angelico. Line 6. Verse 21.
herns and citoles"—a cithern was an ancient stringed instrument, some-
; like a guitar; a citole seems to have been the same as a dulcimer. Especi-
beautiful is the lover's vague consciousness of the hovering presence of his
ove while he is supposed to be writing this poem.

INDEX OF AUTHORS AND SUBJECTS.

CHRONOLOGICAL TABLE

OF

MODERN POETS, ENGLISH AND AMERICAN.

ENGLISH POETS.

	Born	Died
Burns, Robert	1759	1796
Rogers, Samuel	1763	1855
Wordsworth, William	1770	1850
Montgomery, James	1771	1854
Scott, Walter	1771	1832
Coleridge, Samuel Taylor	1772	1834
Southey, Robert	1774	1843
White, J. Blanco	1775	1841
Lamb, Charles	1775	1835
Landor, Walter Savage	1775	1864
Campbell, Thomas	1777	1844
Moore, Thomas	1780	1852
Hunt, Leigh	1784	1859
White, Henry Kirke	1785	1806
Byron, George Gordon Noel	1788	1824
Wolfe, Charles	1791	1823
Shelley, Percy Bysshe	1792	1821
Hemans, Felicia Dorothea	1794	1835
Keats, John	1795	1821

	Born	Died
Hood, Thomas	1798	1845
Macaulay, Thomas Babington	1800	1859
Beddoes, Thomas Lovell	1803	1849
Lytton, Edward Bulwer	1804	1873
Norton, Caroline	1808	1877
Browning, Elizabeth Barrett	1809	1861
Tennyson, Alfred	1809	*
Browning, Robert	1812	*
Clough, Arthur Hugh	1819	1861
Kingsley, Charles	1819	1875
Arnold, Matthew	1822	*
Rossetti, Dante Gabriel	1828	-
Rossetti, Christina	1830	
Ingelow, Jean	1830	
Lytton, Robert (Owen Meredith)	1831	-
Morris, William	1834	
Symonds, John Addington	1840	
Swinburne, Algernon Charles	1843	-
Macdonald, George	?	
Buchanan, Robert	?	

AMERICAN POETS.

	Born	Died
Allston, Washington	1779	1843
Bryant, William Cullen	1794	1878
Emerson, Ralph Waldo	1803	*
Longfellow, Henry Wadsworth	1807	-
Whittier, J. Greenleaf	1807	*
Holmes, Oliver Wendell	1809	1849
Poe, Edgar Allan	1809	1849
Read, T. Buchanan	1822	1872
Taylor, J. Bayard	1825	1878

* Living.

	Born	Died
Hayne, Paul H.	1831	*
Stedman, Edmund Clarence	1833	*
Piatt, John James	1835	*
Aldrich, Thomas Bailey	1836	*
Hay, John (Colonel)	1839	*

* Living.

PRINTING OFFICE OF THE PUBLISHER.

Lightning Source UK Ltd.
Milton Keynes UK
UKHW02f2015040518
322147UK00010B/669/P